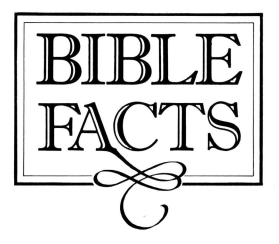

JENNY
ROBERTS

BARNES
&NOBLE
BOOKS
NEW YORK

A QUANTUM BOOK

This hardback edition published
by Barnes & Noble, Inc.,
by arrangement with Quantum Books Ltd
1999 Barnes & Noble Books

ISBN 0-88029-560-0

QUMBIF

M   10   9   8   7   6   5   4

This book was produced by
Quantum Books Ltd
6 Blundell Street
London N7 9BH

Senior Editor Christine Davis
Editor Faith Glasgow

Design Nick Clark, Steven Randall, Daniel Evans
Picture Research Susan Buttenwieser

Picture Manager Joanna Wiese
Art Director Moira Clinch

Special thanks to Grey Matter Design Consultants

Title page picture: St John the Evangelist from
a manuscript of St John's Gospel (C. M. Dixon)

Typeset by Ampersand Typesetting Limited, Bournemouth
Printed in Singapore by Star Standard Industries Pte. Ltd

FOREWORD

The Bible is primarily the repository of the holy writings which form the basis of Judaism and Christianity, inspiring and informing their adherents. But it is much more than that. The Bible is a work of great historical interest, charting the history of the Jewish people over centuries, and the origins and growth of the Christian Church. It is also a considerable work of literature, containing beautiful poetry, exciting narratives, and memorable characters. The influence of the Bible on Western language and thought is incalculable. Without a good knowledge of the Bible much of Western art and literature cannot be fully understood or appreciated.

However despite its continuing status as the best selling book in the world, the Bible is no longer as well known and well read as was once the case. Many people keep a copy on their shelves, but are largely ignorant of its contents, assuming it to be of interest only to those with religious commitments. This book of facts about the Bible and about Bible times, life, lands, and people will send its readers back to the original work with renewed interest and provide a guide through its complexities.

The Bible is not only the best selling book, but also the most widely distributed book in the world. In 1988 the United Bible Society reported that the number of languages and dialects into which complete books of the Bible had been translated had reached 1,907. This includes complete Bibles in 310 languages and New Testaments in 695 languages. Access to the Bible is, at least theoretically, open to up to ninety per cent of the world's population.

The English-speaking world is particularly fortunate in the wealth of different versions of the Bible that are currently available, written in language ranging from the simple eloquence of the early seventeenth century to the most informal modern English.

All quotations in this book are taken from the King James Version. Although subsequent translations have improved on the accuracy of the translation and comprehensibility of the language, the King James is still arguably the most beautifully written and the most memorable of all English Bibles.

JENNY ROBERTS
JUNE 1990

CONTENTS

From the first book of the Bible: the dove brings an olive branch to Noah (Genesis 8:11). This illustration comes from the medieval French Psalter of St Louis

ARCHEOLOGICAL SITES AROUND THE DEAD SEA

Jerusalem   Jericho   Kh. Qumran   En-gedi   Dead Sea   Masada (es-Sebbeh)

O.T. Jericho (T. es-Sultan)   Modern Jericho (Ariha)   N.T. Jericho

−300   −600   −1,000

Cave 3   Cave 1   Cave 11   Cave 5   Cave 2   Cave 6   Kh. Qumran   Cave 4   Dead Sea

0   20 miles

0   20 kilometres

Among the important archeological sites of the Bible lands are the ancient city of Jericho, the spectacular

Herodian fortress of Masada and the famous Qumran caves, where the Dead Sea Scrolls were found in 1947

Special Features

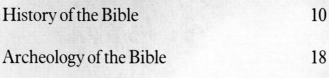

7

Order and Abbreviations
of the Books of the Bible

OLD TESTAMENT

	Abbreviation		*Abbreviation*
Genesis	Gen.	Ecclesiastes	Eccles.
Exodus	Ex.	Song of Solomon	Song
Leviticus	Lev.	Isaiah	Is.
Numbers	Num.	Jeremiah	Jer.
Deuteronomy	Deut.	Lamentations	Lam.
Joshua	Josh.	Ezekiel	Ezek.
Judges	Judg.	Daniel	Dan.
Ruth	Ruth	Hosea	Hos.
1 Samuel	1 Sam.	Joel	Joel
2 Samuel	2 Sam.	Amos	Amos
1 Kings	1 Kgs.	Obadiah	Obad.
2 Kings	2 Kgs.	Jonah	Jon.
1 Chronicles	1 Chron.	Micah	Mic.
2 Chronicles	2 Chron.	Nahum	Nahum
Ezra	Ezra	Habakkuk	Hab.
Nehemiah	Neh.	Zephaniah	Zeph.
Esther	Esth.	Haggai	Hag.
Job	Job	Zechariah	Zech.
Psalms	Ps.	Malachi	Mal.
Proverbs	Prov.		

Order and Abbreviations of the Books of the Bible

NEW TESTAMENT

	Abbreviation		*Abbreviation*
Matthew	Matt.	1 Peter	1 Pet.
Mark	Mark	2 Peter	2 Pet.
Luke	Luke	1 John	1 John
John	John	2 John	2 John
Acts	Acts	3 John	3 John
Romans	Rom.	Jude	Jude
1 Corinthians	1 Cor.	Revelation	Rev.
2 Corinthians	2 Cor.		
Galatians	Gal.		
Ephesians	Eph.		
Philippians	Phil.		
Colossians	Col.		
1 Thessalonians	1 Thess.		
2 Thessalonians	2 Thess.		
1 Timothy	1 Tim.		
2 Timothy	2 Tim.		
Titus	Titus		
Philemon	Philem.		
Hebrews	Heb.		
James	Jas.		

A twelfth-century manuscript from the Armenian Cathedral Library in Jerusalem. The illustration shows Christ entombed

HISTORY OF THE BIBLE

The word Bible *comes, through Latin, from the Greek word* biblia, *meaning "books," which in its turn comes from* byblos, *meaning "papyrus," the material from which books were made. We are used to speaking of the Bible as "a book," but in fact it is a collection of books, of different authorship and written at different times, which have been selected from a wider range of writings to make up the Bible as we know it.*

THE OLD TESTAMENT

The books of the Old Testament were written over centuries and some of them were added to or changed their form over many years. None of the original manuscripts have survived.

We use the word *canon*, meaning "a rule," to denote the list of books that are considered to be the authoritative collection. The Pentateuch, or Five Books of Moses (Genesis, Exodus, Leviticus, Numbers, Deuteronomy), were already considered to be canonical by the time of Ezra and Nehemiah in the fifth century BC. Recognition of the other books came at various times, but by the second century BC they were organized into the twenty-four books that make up the Hebrew Bible. These are the books that the first Christians would have recognized as authoritative, although the manuscripts still existed only as separate scrolls.

The earliest translation of the Hebrew scriptures was the Septuagint, a translation into Greek of all the Old Testament canonical books, and some of those that are regarded by many as apocryphal (*see* p. 12). The Jewish translators (traditionally there were held to be seventy-two of them) started work on the Pentateuch in Alexandria in the first half of the third century BC. The other

canonical books appear to have been translated by the end of the second century BC, and non-canonical books at various times down to the first century AD. The Greek of the Septuagint was much

influenced by the Hebrew original, and the accuracy is sometimes questionable, but the Septuagint was the basis for several subsequent translations. In 382 St Jerome made a Latin translation, called the Vulgate, which is still used by the Roman Catholic Church.

For subsequent translations of the Old Testament taken from the

Hebrew, the source has generally been what is known as the Massoretic text. The Massoretes (transmitters) probably started their work in about AD 500 and did not finish it until the tenth century AD.

THE NEW TESTAMENT

The books of the New Testament were written, in Greek, during the first century AD, but the earliest manuscripts date from the third and fourth centuries AD. There are about 175 manuscripts dating from this period, written on papyrus or parchment, most of them very well preserved. By the middle of the third century AD, parts of the New Testament had been translated into Latin, Syriac, and Coptic.

In the first century AD, and well into the second, there was no conception of a New Testament canon. The Apostolic Fathers of the early Church often quote sayings of Jesus in a form unrelated to any of the four canonical Gospels. Not all of the four Gospels were known to all the Fathers, and there was also various apocryphal material in use. The writings of Paul seem to have been well known and highly valued, but not thought of as scriptural.

The idea of a canon of New Testament scripture started through various heretical movements of the second century AD. A teacher called Marcion broke away from the church in Rome in about 150 AD. He totally rejected the Old Testament and thus felt the need for an authoritative Christian scripture. He devised a canon which consisted of one Gospel (a form of Luke) and ten letters of Paul.

By the second half of the second century AD, the four Gospels were established as authoritative, and by the end of the century the Acts of the Apostles, Paul's letters, and Revelation were also considered canonical. In the third century, a distinction was made by the ecclesiastical historian Eusebius bishop of Caesarea, between acknowledged books (the Gospels, Acts, Paul's letters, 1 Peter, 1 John); disputed books (James, Jude, 2 Peter, 2 and 3 John); and spurious books (Hebrews, and various apocryphal works). There is disagreement over whether Revelation was counted as acknowledged or spurious.

The canon was finally settled for the Eastern Church by the 39th Paschal letter of Athanasius in AD 367, and the West followed after Pope Damasus held a synod in Rome in 382.

Part of one of the leather scrolls found in the Qumran Caves by the Dead Sea in 1947. They are about one thousand years older than any other Hebrew Old Testament manuscript ever found

THE APOCRYPHAL BOOKS

The word *apocrypha* comes from a Greek word meaning "hidden." It is applied to all the books of scripture which are not included in the Protestant Bible, but particularly to the Old Testament books which are included in Roman Catholic versions. There are many other apocryphal books of both Old and New Testaments, which have been rejected as spurious or of doubtful authenticity, and these are now usually referred to as *pseudepigrapha*. The works discussed below are those which are included in the Roman Catholic Old Testament canon, although not all Roman Catholic Bibles contain all of them, and the names of the books sometimes vary.

1 Esdras

This book gives a parallel account of history recorded in the books of Chronicles, Ezra, and Nehemiah. There is also an addition, known as the "Debate of the Three Youths," which is an adaptation from a Persian story. It features Zerubbabel, governor under Darius. He takes part in a debate about the nature of power and uses it to remind Darius of his obligation to allow the rebuilding of the temple.

2 Esdras

This book is also known as "The Apocalypse of Ezra." It derives from a Hebrew source but has been expanded with Christian additions. The book describes seven visions. In the first three visions Ezra asks why God's chosen people have to suffer and be oppressed by other nations. An angel tells him that these things are incomprehensible to human beings, but salvation is close and the Jews will eventually inherit the earth. The fourth vision

The Return of Judith *by Botticelli (1440–1510). The picture shows the Apocryphal heroine and her maid returning to Bethulia with the head of Holofernes, the Assyrian general whom she had killed*

is of a glorious Jerusalem; the next, a symbolic vision of Rome; the sixth is similar to the vision in Daniel 7. The last vision concerns the sacred books that Ezra is to restore.

Tobit

This story dates from the Babylonian exile. It tells of Tobit, a Jew in captivity in Nineveh. He is persecuted for burying the Hebrew dead, and becomes impoverished and blind. He sends his son Tobias to collect a debt. Tobias is guided by the archangel Raphael in disguise. He falls in love with his cousin Sara, whose previous seven bridegrooms have been killed by the demon Asmodeus. Tobias, helped by Raphael, defeats Asmodeus and restores Tobit's sight by means of a fish he has caught in the River Tigris.

Judith

The story dates from a second-century BC Hebrew source. It tells of Judith, a beautiful Jewish widow of Bethulia. Her city is besieged by Nebuchadnezzar's forces, led by the general Holofernes. Judith goes to Holofernes' tent, on the pretext of telling him military secrets. He is taken with her beauty and asks her to dine with him. Judith encourages him to drink freely and, when he is in a drunken sleep, cuts off his head. When she returns to the city and shows the people Holofernes' head, they pursue the enemy, who flee from them.

Additions to Esther

Although most scholars regard these passages as additions to the original Hebrew, some maintain that the Hebrew canonical work is an abbreviated version. The additions include accounts of Mordecai's dream and an interpretation of it; the king's orders for the massacre of Jews and his subsequent edict permitting the Jews to defend themselves; prayers of Mordecai and Esther; and Esther's audience with the king.

Wisdom of Solomon

This work, from an unknown author, has its roots in traditional Jewish Wisdom writing, but was almost certainly composed in Greek. There is evidence of Greek philosophical thought, and Platonic terminology is used. The book praises wisdom and exhorts followers to seek after it. In the second half of the book Jewish history is discussed in the context of the ways in which the Jews have been helped by wisdom.

Ecclesiasticus

This book consists of the wisdom sayings of Joshua ben Sira, who lived in Jerusalem around 180 BC. The translation was made by the author's grandson. The book was well known and highly respected by both Jews and early Christians. It recommends observance of the law and a pious fear of God, and gives practical advice for daily living. The final chapters are devoted to the praise of the patriarchs and heroes of the Old Testament, and of Simon the high priest, who lived about 200 BC.

Baruch

This book is supposedly the work of Baruch, who was the scribe or secretary of the prophet Jeremiah. It is, however, thought to be of composite authorship. It begins with an address by Baruch to the exiles in Babylon, with a prayer of confession, and prayers asking for forgiveness and salvation. The next section speaks in praise of wisdom, and the last chapters are a lament of Jerusalem for the captives, with a final assurance that they will be restored to their home.

Additions to Daniel

The additions to the book of Daniel are derived from the Septuagint. The first addition comes in chapter 3, and consists of the prayer of Azariah (Abednego) in the fiery furnace, in which he praises God's mercy and asks for deliverance; this is followed by the Song of the Three Holy Children, a song of praise uttered as they walk unharmed in the fire, with the refrain "praise and exalt him above all for ever."

The story of Susanna follows from the end of the prophecies of Daniel. It tells of a beautiful and pious woman married to a Babylonian. Two elders of the people see her bathing and, when she rejects their advances, have her falsely accused of adultery. She is condemned to death but Daniel proves that the elders are lying. The people accept Susanna's innocence, and put the elders to death.

The last addition, the story of Bel and the Dragon, is written to mock idolatrous worship. In it Daniel proves to the king that neither the idol Bel nor a dragon (who was also an object of worship) are living gods.

Prayer of Manasses

In 2 Chronicles 13, the reign of Manasseh, son of Hezekiah, is described. He was a worshiper of Baal and other idols, and heavily involved in occult practices. He was captured by the Assyrians and in his affliction prayed to the God of his fathers for release. God heard him and Manasseh was released, subsequently restoring the worship of God to Judah. This book purports to be the prayer of Manasseh when in captivity. It is thought to be Jewish in origin but is not known before the third century AD.

1 and 2 Maccabees

These books are concerned with Jewish history between 175 and 134 BC, and the heroic family of the Maccabees, particularly Judas Maccabeus. It describes their struggles against the Syrian king Antiochus Epiphanes, the Hasmonean wars, and the line of priest-kings that they established. The first book was translated from a Hebrew work, apparently in about 100 BC. The second book is said to be extracted from a work by Jason of Cyrene, who is otherwise unknown. It covers similar ground to the first, but there are various discrepancies and the first is thought to be more accurate.

Susanna Bathing by Albrecht Altdorfer (c. 1480–1538). An illustration of one of the Apocryphal additions to the book of Daniel

Manuscript Bibles

The first attempts at translating parts of the Bible into English began in the seventh century AD. These were not so much translations as poetical works of paraphrase, and no manuscripts have been found. The Venerable Bede is said to have translated the Gospel of John, but again we have no concrete evidence of the work.

One surviving work is that of the **Lindisfarne Gospels**, a beautifully ornamented manuscript, which was written in Latin in about AD 700, but with an English gloss, or interlinear translation, added in about AD 950. About fifty years after this the **West Saxon Gospels** were produced.

During the later Middle English period various parts of the Bible were translated, but the most significant work was that associated with John **Wyclif** (1320–1384), a reformer whose aim was to make the scriptures accessible to the people. There were two versions undertaken in Wyclif's name, parts of which were actually written by the reformer himself. Both were translations from the Latin Vulgate, but the English of the later version, made by John Purvey, one of Wyclif's followers, is far more idiomatic and less archaic.

The Printed Bible

Although Bibles were being printed in Europe from the middle of the fifteenth century, it was not until 1525 that the first Bible to be printed in English appeared. This was the **Tyndale Bible**, produced by William Tyndale, a scholar who, like Wyclif, was determined to make the Bible more available to ordinary lay people. The first part of his Bible, the New Testament, was printed partly in Cologne and partly in Worms in Germany. It was significant, not just as the first printed English Bible, but as the first to be translated from the Greek, rather than Latin. By 1534 Tyndale had produced a complete Pentateuch, the book of Jonah, and other selections from the Old Testament, translated from the Hebrew texts. In 1535 Tyndale was arrested for heresy and executed. His translation has been enormously influential, and much of his work is preserved in the English of the King James Version.

Part of the book of Numbers from the sixteenth-century Tyndale Bible

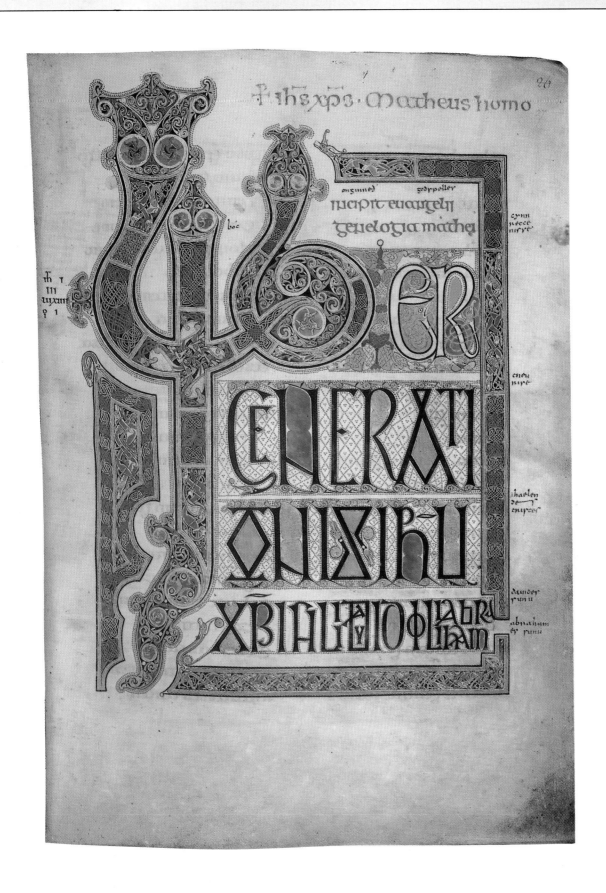

A decorated initial to the Gospel of Matthew, from the eighth-century
Lindisfarne Gospels

At the same time as Tyndale was working on his translation, a complete English Bible was being prepared by **Miles Coverdale**, whose work was published in 1535. Coverdale was ignorant of both Greek and Hebrew and his version was taken partly from the Vulgate, partly from German versions, and partly from Tyndale. His was the first Bible in which non-canonical books were published under the separate heading of "Apocrypha."

In 1537 the English version known as **Matthew's Bible** appeared. Though it claimed to be "truly and purely translated into English by Thomas Matthew" it was in fact the work of John Rogers, a friend and follower of Tyndale, and the Bible was not a new translation but a compilation of Tyndale's and Coverdale's work. Two years later the **Taverner Bible** appeared, but this was no more than a revision of Matthew's Bible.

Another very influential work appeared in 1539: the **Great Bible**, so called because of its large size. This was prepared by Miles Coverdale, commissioned by Thomas Cromwell, and was based on Matthew's Bible, drawing also from Coverdale's earlier work, and from Tyndale. This Bible was authorized by Archbishop Cranmer for distribution in all churches and to all people.

Under Mary Tudor, Protestants were persecuted and Bibles were taken from churches. Many Protestants fled from England, and a group of them who went to Geneva began to produce a Bible there. The **Geneva Bible** was mainly the work of William Whittingham, who based it on the Great Bible but with attention paid to Hebrew scholarship. This was the first Bible where the chapters were divided into verses. When Elizabeth took over the throne, England became safe for Protestants again, but the work continued to be centered in Geneva. It appeared in 1560, with a dedication to Elizabeth, but did not receive official endorsement. Instead the Archbishop of Canterbury, Matthew Parker, ordered a revision of the work, the **Bishops' Bible**, which appeared in 1568, with a revised version in 1572. This revised version was to be the basis for the King James Version.

Just as Protestants had fled to the Continent in Mary's reign, Roman Catholics fled in Elizabeth's. A group of these who had settled in France published a New Testament in Rheims in 1582 and an Old Testament in Douay in 1610. The **Douay Version** is mainly a translation from the Vulgate.

The **Authorized** or **King James Version** was commissioned by James I. Work started on it in 1604 and it was printed in 1611. The basis for the translation was the Bishops' Bible but the translators consulted the Greek and Hebrew texts, and followed Tyndale, Matthew's, Coverdale, or the Geneva versions when it seemed to them that these translations were more accurate. The first edition was marred by typographical errors; subsequent editions have corrected these and modernized spelling and punctuation. The King James Bible became the standard version for Protestants all over the English-speaking world. It is still much used today, and nearly all modern translations are indebted to it.

In 1870 work on a **Revised Version** of the King James was started, organized by the Church of England but involving other denominations and American Bible scholars. The complete work was published in 1885 in England, with the **American Standard Version** published six years later.

Some twentieth-century versions which deserve mention include the **Revised Standard Version** of 1952, the Roman Catholic **Jerusalem Bible** of 1966, the **New International Bible** of 1978, and the best-selling and very popular modern version, the **Good News Bible** of 1976.

SPECIALLY NAMED EDITIONS

Some Bibles have been given special names because of a typographical error or peculiarity of vocabulary. Some of these are listed below:

Adulterous Bible: *see* **Wicked Bible**

Breeches Bible: Another name for the Geneva Bible. Genesis 3:7 says that Adam and Eve "sowed figge-tree leaves together and made themselves breeches."

Bug Bible: Another name for the Coverdale Bible in which Psalm 91:5 reads, "Thou shalt not need to be afrayd for eny bugges by night."

Discharge Bible: An 1806 edition in which 1 Timothy 5:21 says, "I discharge thee ... that thou observe these things," instead of "I charge thee."

Ears to Ear Bible: An edition of 1810, where Matthew 13:43 reads, "Who hath ears to ear, let him hear."

Idle Shepherd: An 1809 edition in which the "idol shepherd" of Zechariah 11:17 becomes "the idle shepherd."

Murderers Bible: An 1801 edition where Jude 16 reads, "These are murderers, complainers ..," instead of "murmurers."

Placemakers Bible: The 1562 second edition of the Geneva Bible, where Matthew 5:9 reads, "Blessed are the placemakers."

Printers' Bible: An early eighteenth-century edition where Psalm 119:161 says, "printers have persecuted me without a cause," instead of "princes."

Rebekah's Camels Bible: An 1823 edition which gives Genesis 24:61 as "Rebekah arose, and her camels," instead of "her damsels."

Standing Fishes Bible: An edition of 1806 where Ezekiel 47:10 has "And it shall come to pass that the fishes shall stand on it," instead of "fishers."

To Remain Bible: A Bible printed in Cambridge in 1805. A proofreader queried a comma and the editor penciled in "to remain"; as a result, Galatians 4:29 read, "he that was born after the flesh persecuted him that was born after the spirit to remain, even so it is now."

Treacle Bible: A name for the Bishops' Bible because of its use of "tryacle" for "balm," as in Jeremiah 8:22, "Is there no tryacle in Gilead?"

Unrighteous Bible: A Cambridge edition of 1653. In 1 Corinthians 6:9 the word "not" was omitted, leaving "the unrighteous shall inherit the kingdom of God"; and Romans 6:13 read, "Neither yield ye your members as instruments of righteousness unto sin," instead of "unrighteousness."

Vinegar Bible: An Oxford edition printed in 1717 where the heading in Luke 20 reads "Parable of the Vinegar," instead of "Vineyard."

Wicked Bible: Also called **Adulterous Bible**. An edition of 1632 in which the word "not" was omitted from the seventh commandment (Ex. 20:14).

Wife-hater Bible: An 1810 edition where Luke 14:26 says, "If any man come to me, and hates not his father ... and his own wife also," instead of "his own life."

ARCHEOLOGY OF THE BIBLE

The archeology of the Bible covers two major areas of research. There is biblical archeology, a branch within the general science of archeology, in which the geographical areas selected for research are the Bible lands and surrounding areas. Then there is the archeology of Bible texts, where the research is centered on actual biblical manuscripts. Both are covered in this account.

BIBLICAL ARCHEOLOGY

Biblical archeology is primarily a source of historical information. Taken in conjunction with the Bible itself and other evidence, it helps us to ascertain and understand the sequence of biblical events, and to build up a picture of what life was like in Bible lands in those times.

Many of the problems of biblical archeology are those that are common to all archeology of antiquity: the arbitrariness of which items happen to survive, and the fact that organic materials such as leather, wood, and textiles generally fail to survive over such huge time-scales. The sheer vastness of potential sites for investigation, combined with limited resources, also presents problems. Further difficulties are raised by the inaccessibility of many sites because they are inhabited; or because they are sacred to Christians, Jews, and/or Muslims; or because of political tensions in the area. Despite these difficulties, impressive finds have been made and, as the science of archeology has become more exact, these have contributed greatly to Bible scholarship.

Mesopotamia

The area known as the Fertile Crescent stretches from Sumeria at the top of the Persian Gulf, up the

This tablet, found in Diyala in Iraq, shows daily life scenes from Mesopotamia. It dates from around 2600–2500 BC

Euphrates and the Tigris through Babylonia and Assyria, westwards along the southern edge of the Armenian mountains, southwards through Syria and Lebanon to the Jordan Valley, and down to the

Dead Sea. This is the route that **Abraham** took, and it could be said that the same route was taken by Middle Eastern civilization. The archeological sites in Mesopotamia are rich sources of evidence for their long history of occupation by technically and culturally advanced peoples with well-developed social organization.

The ancient civilizations of Assyria and Babylonia dominated this area for centuries. Although both were occupied from prehistoric times, probably the most interesting archeological work has been concentrated on the period when the city-states of these empires were flourishing.

Excavation on the site of the city of **Nineveh** began in the middle of the nineteenth century, and it was not long before reliefs and inscriptions were found which clearly came from the palaces of Sennacherib and Ashurbanipal. Huge numbers of inscribed tablets were subsequently found, providing invaluable information about Assyrian literature and civilization.

The site at Calah, south of Nineveh, has revealed the ruins of temple-towers (ziggurats), and enough of the remains of the temple of Nabu and the palace of Ashurnasirpal II (879 BC) to enable scholars to construct accurate plans of the original buildings. Sculptures, ivories, and weapons were found in the outer town, and are thought to be booty captured by the Assyrian army.

Babylon was always a center of interest to explorers hoping to find the remains of the Tower of Babel. These have never been found although some have identified it with the ruins of a ziggurat found a few miles south-west. A tablet has also been found, dated 229 BC, which describes a tower restored by **Nebuchadnezzar**, and some of the actual building was discovered in 1899. Excavations on the site of Babylon from the mid-nineteenth century to the present have uncovered much of the city of Nebuchadnezzar's reign. The city was surrounded by a double wall, and entrance to the inner city was through various large gateways. The most magnificent was the Ishtar Gate, the bricks of which were glazed and decorated with pictures of animals. Remains have also been found of temples

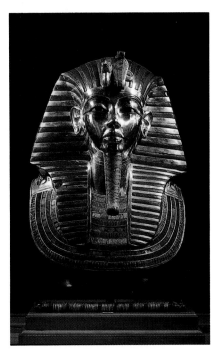

The mask of Tutankhamun. One of the treasures discovered in the tomb of the young pharoah, who reigned in the middle of the fourteenth century BC

dedicated to Ishtar and Marduk, and part of the palace throne room.

The site of the ancient city of **Ur** has revealed far older artifacts than any other site of the region. In the 1920s, the English archeologist Sir Leonard Woolley discovered a royal cemetery dating back to 2500 BC and containing the remains of gold and silver beakers, jewelry, weapons, and musical instruments.

The city of Mari is not mentioned in the Bible, but was one of the most important of the Mesopotamian city-states. Excavations have revealed a huge palace there, dating from about 1775 BC and containing various treasures including over twenty thousand cuneiform texts.

Egypt
The other main route for the advance of ideas and technology into Palestine was from Egypt. The

trade routes from the Nile delta to the East followed the Mediterranean coast and then turned northward through **Canaan**, and there is plenty of archeological evidence of Egyptian influence on Bible lands. The sites in Egypt are even more impressive than those of Mesopotamia because what survived is not arbitrary and accidental. The Egyptians wanted their rulers to have luxury in the next world, so they stocked their tombs with the costliest artifacts possible, and they did so with the intention of preservation.

Archeology in Egypt began when Napoleon invaded the area in 1798, and much of the best work has been carried out by French archeologists, though it was the Englishman Howard Carter who discovered Tutankhamun's tomb in 1922. Tutankhamun died within a hundred years of **Moses'** lifetime, and from the extraordinary treasures of his tomb we can discover what it was like for Moses to grow up in an Egyptian palace. It also throws light on the construction of the tabernacle and the Ark of the Covenant, for elaborate tent-shrines and wooden chests were found in the tomb.

Another discovery that relates to Old Testament accounts was that of the ruins of temples and palaces at Tanis, now San el-Hagar, in the Nile delta. The buildings dated from the ninth century BC, but many of the blocks were inscribed with the name of Rameses II who lived four hundred years earlier. These blocks are thought to have been transported from Qantir, eighteen miles to the south, where the remains of a city were discovered. This city is believed to be Pi-Ramesse, or the Raamses that the Israelites were forced to build by their Egyptian taskmasters (Ex. 1:11).

Canaan

Compared with the powerful empires to the east and south-west, the Israelites were a rough peasant people, with a less developed culture in the form of literature, art, or military or administrative skills.

There are particular difficulties with some of the areas that conceal potentially valuable information. **Damascus** has been continuously occupied on the same site for thousands of years, and **Jerusalem** also dates back to ancient times. Unfortunately, because both are now huge modern cities, major excavations are not possible.

Jericho, however, is another very ancient city which, being uninhabited, has been available for archeological research. Work began in 1868, but the most interesting research was carried out by Kathleen Kenyon in the 1950s. She found that the remains of walls previously discovered and thought to be those destroyed by **Joshua** were in fact the ruins of buildings destroyed by earthquake before 1500 BC. Pottery, weapons, and furniture of this period have also been found on the site. Nothing has been found of the city that the Israelites conquered under Joshua, but ruins have been found. nearby of the winter palace of **Herod the Great**, built in Jericho about 100 BC.

Such excavation as has been possible in Jerusalem has also yielded evidence of the many magnificent buildings erected by Herod the Great, particularly the temple, which was ruined in AD 70. However, probably the most interesting Herodian remains have been found in Masada, west of the Dead Sea. On this isolated rock Herod built a huge fortress and two palaces. Israeli archeologists, working in the 1960s, made extraordinary discoveries at Masada. Reservoirs had been cut into the rock, with channels and aqueducts to supply water to the

A reconstruction of Solomon's Temple at Jerusalem. The construction of the building is described in 1 Kings 6–7 and 2 Chronicles 3–4

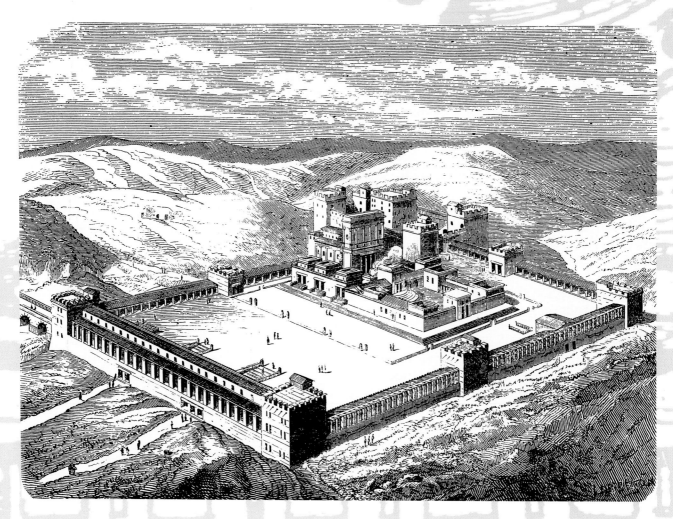

Top aerial view of Masada, the site of the
fortress and palace built in the rocks near the
Dead Sea by Herod the Great

Above The storerooms belonging to the
fortress

fortress. A strong double wall
enclosed barracks, storerooms,
and the two palaces, one built for
administrative and official
purposes and the other as a
pleasure palace. Some of the most
interesting discoveries were from a
later period, when Masada was
occupied by Jewish zealots who
were using the fortress as a
stronghold against the Romans in
AD 66–73. The remains of a
synagogue and ritual baths were
found, besides fragments of leather
scrolls, some bearing biblical texts.

ARCHEOLOGY OF BIBLE TEXTS

In order to survive for very long
periods of time, texts and
documents need to be written on
stone or clay. These are slow to
produce and extremely difficult to
transport, so are characteristic of
settled civilizations. The advanced
societies surrounding the Palestine
area left a great deal of writing
behind. The library of
Ashurbanipal at **Nineveh**,
discovered in the 1850s, is an
excellent source of information on
Assyrian culture and contains
among other things the Epic of
Gilgamesh. This story is written on
a clay tablet dating back to at least
1600 BC and tells the story of a great
flood, with remarkable similarities
to the Genesis story. Mari (*see*
p. 19) was another source of
interesting clay tablets, giving an
insight into political, military,
religious, and social life in the
region.

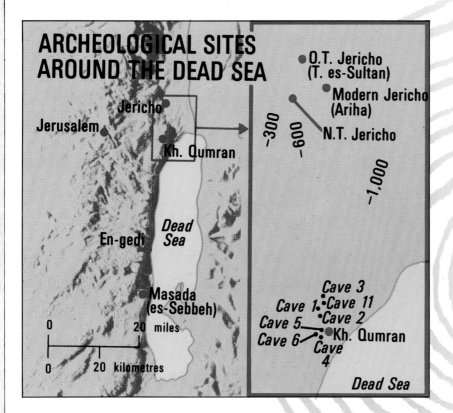

ARCHEOLOGICAL SITES AROUND THE DEAD SEA

Jerusalem

Jericho

Kh. Qumran

En-gedi

Dead Sea

Masada (es-Sebbeh)

0   20 miles

0   20 kilometres

O.T. Jericho (T. es-Sultan)

Modern Jericho (Ariha)

N.T. Jericho

-300

-600

-1,000

Cave 3
Cave 1 Cave 11
Cave 5   Cave 2
Cave 6   Kh. Qumran
Cave 4

Dead Sea

The location of the Qumran Caves, and Khirbet Qumran, the region where archeologists discovered the holy books and the community dwelling of the old Jewish Essene sect

The Dead Sea Scrolls

The Hebrew people did not dwell securely enough or for long enough anywhere to leave much writing in a durable form. Most biblical texts have come down to us as a result of repeated copying in a perishable medium such as leather or papyrus. This can give rise to doubts about the historical authenticity of the texts. The greatest archeological breakthrough in this area has undoubtedly been the discovery of the Dead Sea Scrolls.

THE QUMRAN CAVES Qumran is the name of a wadi and a nearby ruin (Khirbet Qumran) just north-west of the Dead Sea. Early in 1947 a shepherd chanced upon a cave in the cliff face and discovered some jars containing bundles of old cloth and rolls of leather with writing on them. He returned a little later with friends and discovered more of the same.

The rolls went through many hands before they finally made their way to the American School of Oriental Research in Jerusalem, where an American scholar, John Trever, identified them as scrolls of Hebrew texts and realized that one of them was a copy of the book of Isaiah, which appeared to be older than any known Hebrew manuscript.

The results of Trever's research were made public in April 1948, and in the following years archeologists explored all the caves in the area. More scrolls were found, although these were mainly fragments, not so well preserved as they had not been kept in jars. Between 1951 and 1956 the archeologists turned their attention to the Khirbet Qumran site and excavated a building there which appeared to have belonged to a community of people. The evidence suggested that they had occupied the site for two centuries up to AD 68, with a thirty-year break between about AD 4 and 34.

The community seemed likely to have been a branch of the Jewish Essene sect, and it was clear that

the scrolls found in the caves had been their property. Pottery found in the caves and the ruins were identical, and jars found in the ruins were similar to those which had contained the scrolls. Roman troops, marching through Palestine to suppress the Jewish revolt, would have reached the Dead Sea region in about AD 68. The Essene community at Qumran probably hid their scrolls at that point, and were either killed or fled from the area.

THE BIBLE SCROLLS The manuscript that Trever identified as the book of Isaiah was a roll of leather twenty-four inches long and ten inches high. It was made of seventeen sheets sewn together end to end, and covered with fifty-four columns of Hebrew text. It has been confirmed that this scroll is around a thousand years older than any existing Hebrew manuscript. When compared with the Massoretic texts, various differences were found, but on the whole there were no major changes and the discovery tended to give greater authority to the accuracy of the Jewish copyists.

Much can be derived about the Essenes' theology from the biblical commentaries. They thought of themselves as the righteous remnant of Israel, and rejected the Hasmonean dynasty. They spoke of someone whom they called "The Teacher of Righteousness," but he appears to have been a leader and teacher of the sect rather than a Messiah figure. Members of the sect spent many hours in study of the law, and their interpretation of it was stricter than that of the Pharisees. Their interpretation of scripture was apocalyptic and they lived in expectation of the "end-time". They were expecting the last days to signal the end of the "epoch of wickedness" and awaited the coming of a Messiah of David's line who would be a warrior prince, leading the faithful of Israel to victory over the "sons of darkness." They also awaited a judgment and a general resurrection at the end-time.

Eventually fragments of every canonical book of the Hebrew Old Testament except for the book of Esther, as well as some of the apocryphal books, were found in the caves. The manuscripts date from the last few centuries BC to the beginning of the first century AD. Most are in Hebrew but some are in Aramaic. They include both texts of the kind that the Massoretic scholars would have used and the text underlying the Septuagint. There are also texts similar to the Hebrew Pentateuch used by the Samaritans. The texts are now all in the Israel Museum in Jerusalem and are still in the process of being studied and evaluated.

THE ESSENES As well as the Bible texts found, the library in the Qumran caves included large numbers of texts which related to the life and beliefs of the community who lived there. Together with the remains of buildings and artifacts found in the ruins of Khirbet Qumran, they have enabled us to build up a picture of the "people of the scrolls" who lived there.

The non-biblical texts included Bible commentaries, books of rules for community life, and regulations concerning worship. The evidence from these is close enough to what has been learned about the Essene sect from contemporary writers such as Josephus, Pliny, and Philo

for most scholars to be convinced that the Qumran community were Essenes. This sect flourished during the period from about 100 BC to AD 100 and are of particular interest because of some similarities between their beliefs and practices and those of the early Christian Church.

Like other Essene communities the people at Qumran lived a simple, rigorously disciplined, and austere life. The Essenes believed in the practice of hospitality and communal ownership of property. There was a novitiate of two years before anyone could join the community; admission was preceded by a ritual ablution or purification in water; and fellowship meals were held in

secret. Although there are obviously some parallels to Christian rituals of baptism and communion here, there are significant differences and the Essene rituals did not have the sacramental significance of Christian ones.

Below One of the caves at Qumran, where the Dead Sea Scrolls were found

Inset The leather scrolls were hidden inside pottery jars, which helped to preserve them

A sixteenth-century depiction of preparations on the hill of Calvary, by Lucas van Valkenborch (c. 1530–97)

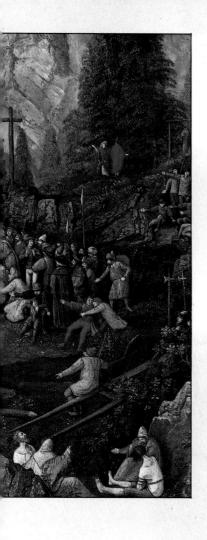

Books of the Bible

The following section gives a brief account of the historical background and the contents of each book of the Old and New Testament. The order followed is that of the Protestant canon. The books of the Protestant Apocrypha are discussed elsewhere.

Books of the Old Testament

HEBREW CLASSIFICATION

HATORAH (THE LAW)

Genesis
Exodus
Leviticus
Numbers
Deuteronomy

HANEVI'IM (THE PROPHETS)

Joshua
Judges
Samuel
Kings
Isaiah
Jeremiah
Ezekiel
Hosea
Joel
Amos
Obadiah
Jonah
Micah
Nahum
Habakkuk
Zephaniah
Haggai
Zechariah
Malachi

HAKETUVIM (THE WRITINGS)

Psalms
Proverbs
Job
Song of Solomon
Ruth
Lamentations
Ecclesiastes
Esther
Daniel
Ezra
Nehemiah
Chronicles

PROTESTANT CLASSIFICATION

PENTATEUCH

Genesis
Exodus
Leviticus
Numbers
Deuteronomy

HISTORIES

Joshua
Judges
Ruth
1 & 2 Samuel (1 & 2 Kings)
1 & 2 Kings (3 & 4 Kings)
1 & 2 Chronicles
Ezra
Nehemiah
Esther

WISDOM WRITINGS

Job
Psalms
Proverbs
Ecclesiastes
Song of Solomon

MAJOR PROPHETS

Isaiah
Jeremiah
Lamentations
Ezekiel
Daniel

MINOR PROPHETS

Hosea
Joel
Amos
Obadiah
Jonah
Micah
Nahum
Habakkuk
Zephaniah
Haggai
Zechariah
Malachi

PROTESTANT APOCRYPHA

1 & 2 Esdras
Tobit
Judith
Additions to Esther
Wisdom of Solomon
Ecclesiasticus
Baruch
Additions to Daniel
Prayer of Manasses
1 & 2 Maccabees

ROMAN CATHOLIC CANON

Italicised books are unique to this list

Genesis
Exodus
Leviticus
Numbers
Deuteronomy
Josue
Judges
1 & 2 Kings
3 & 4 Kings
1 & 2 Paralipomenon (1 & 2 Chronicles)
1 Esdras (Ezra)
2 Esdras (Nehemiah)
Tobias
Judith
Esther
Job
Psalms
Proverbs
Ecclesiastes
Canticle of Canticles
Wisdom
Ecclesiasticus
Isaias
Jeremias
Lamentations
Baruch
Ezechiel
Daniel
Osee
Joel
Amos
Abdias
Jonas
Micheas
Nahum
Habacuc
Sophonias
Haggeus
Zacharias
Malachias
1 & 2 Machabees

The Chronology of the Old Testament

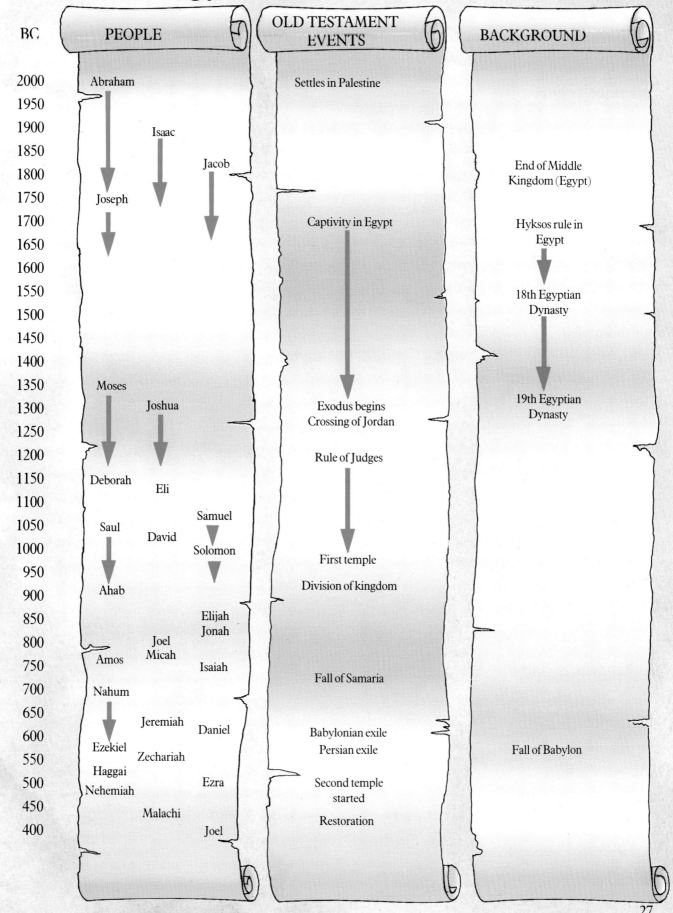

BC	PEOPLE	OLD TESTAMENT EVENTS	BACKGROUND
2000	Abraham	Settles in Palestine	
1950			
1900	Isaac		
1850			
1800	Jacob		End of Middle Kingdom (Egypt)
1750	Joseph		
1700		Captivity in Egypt	Hyksos rule in Egypt
1650			
1600			
1550			18th Egyptian Dynasty
1500			
1450			
1400			
1350	Moses		
1300	Joshua	Exodus begins Crossing of Jordan	19th Egyptian Dynasty
1250			
1200		Rule of Judges	
1150	Deborah Eli		
1100			
1050	Samuel		
1000	Saul David Solomon	First temple	
950			
900	Ahab	Division of kingdom	
850	Elijah Jonah		
800	Joel Micah		
750	Amos Isaiah		
700	Nahum	Fall of Samaria	
650			
600	Jeremiah Daniel	Babylonian exile	
550	Ezekiel Zechariah	Persian exile	Fall of Babylon
500	Haggai Ezra	Second temple started	
450	Nehemiah		
400	Malachi Joel	Restoration	

GENESIS

Traditionally believed to have been written by **Moses**, Genesis is now thought to be a work of composite authorship, written at various times, although there is no general agreement as to dates.

The book can be divided into two sections, chapters 1–11 and 12–50. The early chapters deal with prehistory. Here we have the account of God's creation of the world and his dealings with the first people: **Adam** and **Eve**, **Cain** and **Abel**, **Noah** and the flood, the tower of Babel. The rest of the book is the history of the patriarchs: **Abraham**, **Isaac**, **Jacob**, and **Joseph**. In the stories of these men, their travels, and their families, there is an emphasis on God's promises to his chosen people. At the end of the book, Joseph's family is in the land of **Egypt**, where the oppression of the Israelites began.

In the beginning God created the heaven and the earth. And the earth was without form, and void; and darkness was upon the face of the deep. And the Spirit of God moved upon the face of the waters. And God said, Let there be light: and there was light. (Gen. 1:1–3)

EXODUS

Exodus, too, was originally thought to be the work of **Moses**, but it now seems probable that it was written by various authors and at times ranging from the eighth to the second century BC.

The first half of the book tells the story of the deliverance of the Hebrew people from oppression in **Egypt**, and their journey to **Canaan** – the promised land. These chapters cover God's promise to Moses of "a land flowing with milk and honey"; the nine plagues that were visited on Egypt; the origin of the Passover; and the wanderings of the people in the desert under Moses' leadership. The second half of the book is an account of the Law that Moses received from God on Mount **Sinai**, and includes the Ten Commandments.

I am the Lord thy God, which have brought thee out of the land of Egypt, out of the house of bondage. Thou shalt have no other gods before me. (Ex. 20:2–3)

Above *An illustration on a sixteenth-century Italian earthenware plate. It depicts the institution of the Passover, described in Exodus 12*

Left *Inspired by the account in Genesis of God's creation of the world, this illustration shows the sun, moon, and stars; land and sea; Adam and Eve and the animals, including the serpent*

Right *God Writing the Tablets of the Covenant by William Blake (1757–1838). The picture shows Moses bowing before God on Mount Sinai (Ex. 33: 20–34: 8)*

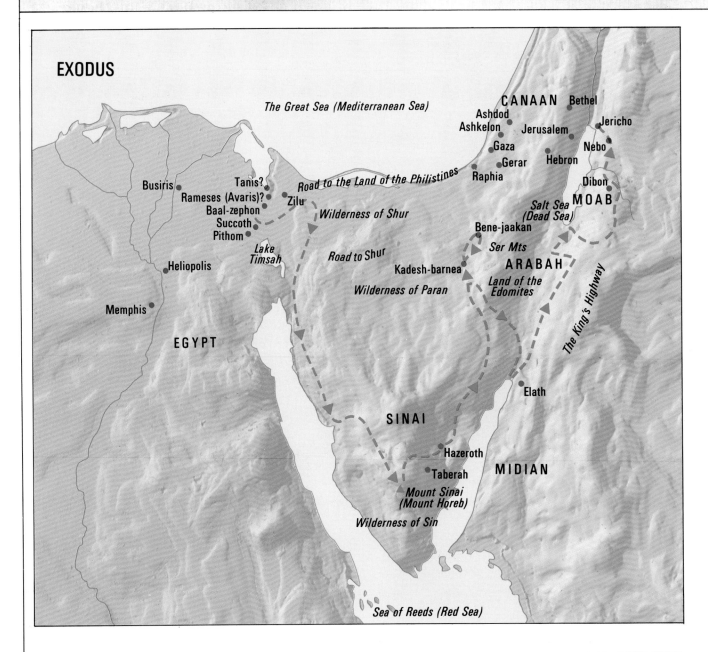

EXODUS

The route taken by the Israelites
on their journey from Egypt to
the promised land of Canaan

*The longest book in the King James Version of
the Bible is the book of Psalms; the shortest is
the third letter of John, with only 294 words in
fourteen verses. John's second letter has only
thirteen verses, but four more words.*

LEVITICUS

Originally also thought to have been written by **Moses**, Leviticus differs from the first two books of the Old Testament in that it appears to have been derived from only one document. It was probably written in the fifth century BC.

The content of the book is almost entirely Jewish ritual law. It begins with laws concerning offerings and sacrifices, and goes on to outline the form of service for the tabernacle. There follow laws about what is clean and unclean; much of the Jewish dietary law is to be found here. The rest of the book details laws concerning marriage, morality, the priesthood, and other matters. Leviticus includes instructions for observing all the major Jewish holy days.

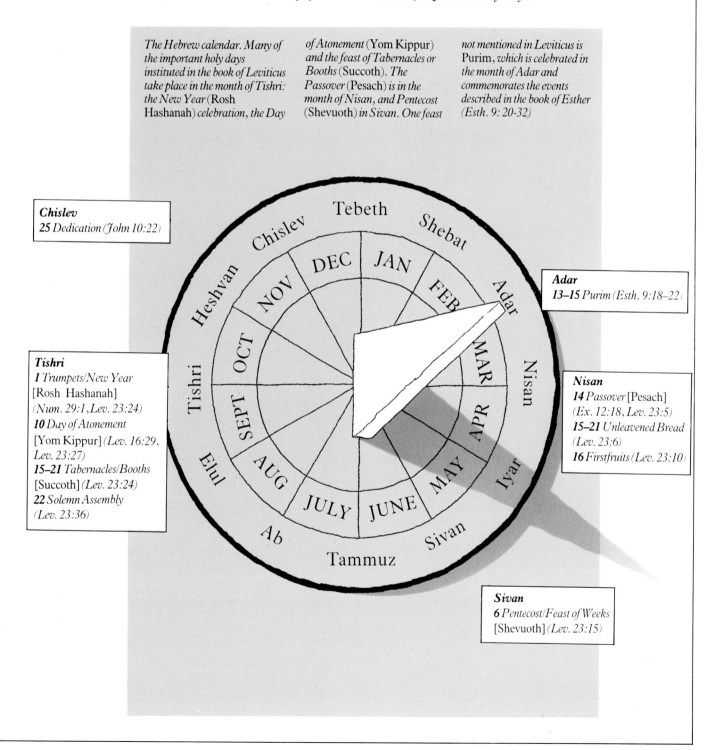

The Hebrew calendar. Many of the important holy days instituted in the book of Leviticus take place in the month of Tishri: the New Year (Rosh Hashanah) celebration, the Day of Atonement (Yom Kippur) and the feast of Tabernacles or Booths (Succoth). The Passover (Pesach) is in the month of Nisan, and Pentecost (Shevuoth) in Sivan. One feast not mentioned in Leviticus is Purim, which is celebrated in the month of Adar and commemorates the events described in the book of Esther (Esth. 9: 20-32)

Chislev
25 *Dedication (John 10:22)*

Tishri
1 *Trumpets/New Year* [Rosh Hashanah] *(Num. 29:1, Lev. 23:24)*
10 *Day of Atonement* [Yom Kippur] *(Lev. 16:29, Lev. 23:27)*
15–21 *Tabernacles/Booths* [Succoth] *(Lev. 23:24)*
22 *Solemn Assembly (Lev. 23:36)*

Adar
13–15 *Purim (Esth. 9:18–22)*

Nisan
14 *Passover* [Pesach] *(Ex. 12:18, Lev. 23:5)*
15–21 *Unleavened Bread (Lev. 23:6)*
16 *Firstfruits (Lev. 23:10)*

Sivan
6 *Pentecost/Feast of Weeks* [Shevuoth] *(Lev. 23:15)*

NUMBERS

The material of Numbers appears to date from Mosaic times, and was traditionally attributed to **Moses**, but was probably written several centuries later.

Covering some of the same ground as Exodus, the book records the life of the Hebrew people between their stay at Mount **Sinai** and their arrival at the borders of **Canaan**. Numbers contains the sending out of spies into Canaan; details of further laws given by God via Moses; the Hebrews' struggles against the various peoples who warred against them; the deaths of **Aaron** and **Miriam**. The book is so named because of the various numberings and censuses of the people which are described.

The Lord bless thee, and keep thee: the Lord make his face shine upon thee, and be gracious unto thee: the Lord lift up his countenance upon thee, and give thee peace. (Num. 6:24–26)

DEUTERONOMY

Deuteronomy is now supposed to have been written in the seventh century BC, although some of it appears to date from an earlier period. It, too, was originally held to have been written by **Moses**.

The first thirty chapters of Deuteronomy consist of three addresses given by Moses to the people. In these he reminds them of the great things that God has done for them, calls them to commit themselves completely to the covenant that God has made with them, and outlines various aspects of the Law. The remainder of the book deals with the final days of Moses: his last words, his handing of the leadership to **Joshua**, his final blessing, death, and burial.

Hear, O Israel: the Lord our God is one Lord: and thou shalt love the Lord thy God with all thine heart, and with all thy soul, and with all thy might. (Deut. 6:4-5)

JOSHUA

Similar in language to Deuteronomy, the book of **Joshua** was probably written around the same period, although it incorporates writings dating from a much earlier period.

The book continues the story of the Israelites' journey to the promised land with accounts of the invasion and settlement of **Canaan** under Joshua's leadership. Much of the book deals with military campaigns, notably the conquest of **Jericho**, although there is also some spiritual content. The book ends with Joshua's death.

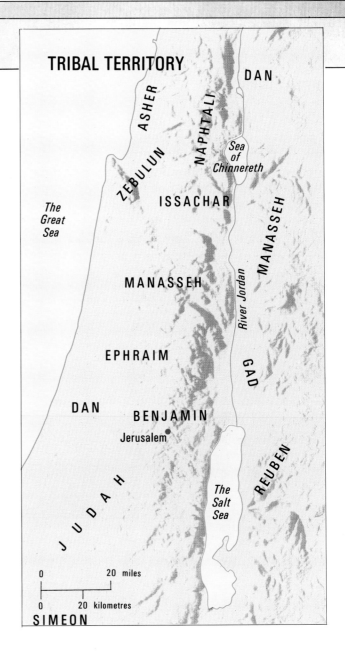

TRIBAL TERRITORY

Above The division of the land of Canaan between the tribes of Israel, as described in the book of Joshua

Right The Fall of Jericho by Jean Fouquet (c. 1425–80). represents a fanciful and medievalized view of the ancient city. The only attempt at historical accuracy seems to be the depiction of priests with ram's horn trumpets, followed by priests carrying the ark of the Lord

JUDGES

Traditionally thought to have been written by the prophet **Samuel**, Judges was probably edited into its final form around the sixth century BC.

Judges continues the account of the settlement of **Canaan** after the death of **Joshua**. The judges of the title were the military and spiritual leaders of Israel,

who included **Deborah**, **Gideon**, and **Samson**. The book is largely concerned with the constant battles between the new settlers and the former inhabitants of the land. There is also emphasis on the increasing lawlessness of the Hebrew people during this period.

RUTH

Although it was long believed to have been written by the prophet **Samuel**, the book of Ruth contains no clues as to authorship and was probably written at least five hundred years after the events described.

The book is a simple narrative set in the time of the judges. It tells the story of the young Moabite widow **Ruth** who leaves her home to accompany her mother-in-law **Naomi**, who is returning to **Bethlehem**. Ruth becomes a gleaner in the fields of **Boaz**, a rich land-owner who is a relative of Naomi's, and eventually marries him.

I ntreat me not to leave thee, or to return from following after thee: for whither thou goest, I will go; and where thou lodgest, I will lodge: thy people shall be my people, and thy God my God: where thou diest, will I die, and there will I be buried. (Ruth 1:16–17)

SAMUEL

The two books of Samuel were treated as one book until the fifteenth century. The material is thought to be drawn from a collection of narrative sources and is unlikely to have been edited into its final form before the fifth century BC.

The two books cover about a century of history. The first seven chapters deal with **Samuel**'s early years and the Philistines' oppression of Israel. The next eight chapters describe the people's demand for a king, Samuel's anointing of **Saul**, and Saul's reign. The rest of the first book deals with **David**'s rise, his exile as a fugitive from Saul, and the death of Saul and his sons. The second book tells of the reign of David.

Saul and Jonathan were lovely and pleasant in their lives, and in their death they were not divided: they were swifter than eagles, they were stronger than lions. (2 Sam. 1:23)

KINGS

These two books were originally one, forming a whole with the books of Samuel. The final editing cannot have taken place before the fifth century BC, although some of the narrative was probably written at an earlier period.

The first book of Kings begins with the last days and death of **David**. The reign of his son **Solomon** is described, including the building of the temple. Kings ch. 1 v. 11: 29–37 deals with the division of the king-dom, and from chapter twelve onward the tribes are

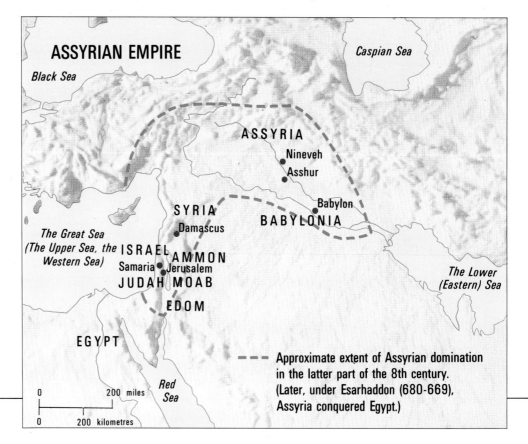

The Assyrian Empire and surrounding regions. Assyria was an immensely powerful nation in Old Testament times, and one of Israel's traditional enemies

ASSYRIAN EMPIRE

Black Sea

Caspian Sea

ASSYRIA
Nineveh
Asshur

Babylon

SYRIA
Damascus

BABYLONIA

The Great Sea
(The Upper Sea, the
Western Sea)

ISRAEL
AMMON
Samaria Jerusalem
JUDAH MOAB
EDOM

The Lower
(Eastern) Sea

EGYPT

0   200 miles

Red
Sea

0   200 kilometres

Approximate extent of Assyrian domination
in the latter part of the 8th century.
(Later, under Esarhaddon (680-669),
Assyria conquered Egypt.)

A manuscript illustration showing the construction of the temple at Jerusalem under the orders of Solomon. Apart from some details, like the gold inlay, the picture owes more to the artist's imagination than to the description in 1 Kings 6 and 7

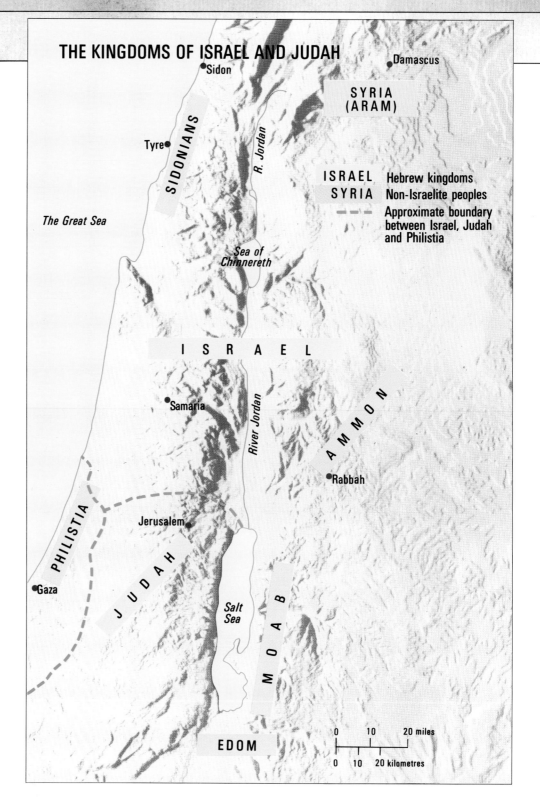

THE KINGDOMS OF ISRAEL AND JUDAH

*The division of the kingdom into
the northern kingdom of Israel
and the southern kingdom
of Judah, as described in
1 Kings 11*

Damascus

Sidon

**SYRIA
(ARAM)**

Tyre

R. Jordan

SIDONIANS

ISRAEL Hebrew kingdoms
SYRIA Non-Israelite peoples
— — Approximate boundary
between Israel, Judah
and Philistia

The Great Sea

*Sea of
Chinnereth*

I S R A E L

Samaria

River Jordan

A M M O N

Rabbah

PHILISTIA

Jerusalem

J U D A H

Gaza

*Salt
Sea*

M O A B

0	10	20 miles
0	10	20 kilometres

EDOM

divided into the kingdoms of Israel and **Judah**. Much
of the remainder of the books is concerned with the
military successes and defeats of the various kings,
and their lapses into idolatry. The prophets **Elijah**
and **Elisha** figure largely in these accounts. The
second book ends with the defeat of Judah and the
beginning of the Babylonian exile.

*And behold, the Lord passed by, and a great and strong
wind rent the mountains, and brake in pieces the rocks
before the Lord; but the Lord was not in the wind: and
after the wind an earthquake; but the Lord was not in the
earthquake: and after the earthquake a fire; but the Lord
was not in the fire: and after the fire a still small voice.
(1 Kgs. 19:11–12)*

Kings of Israel and Judah

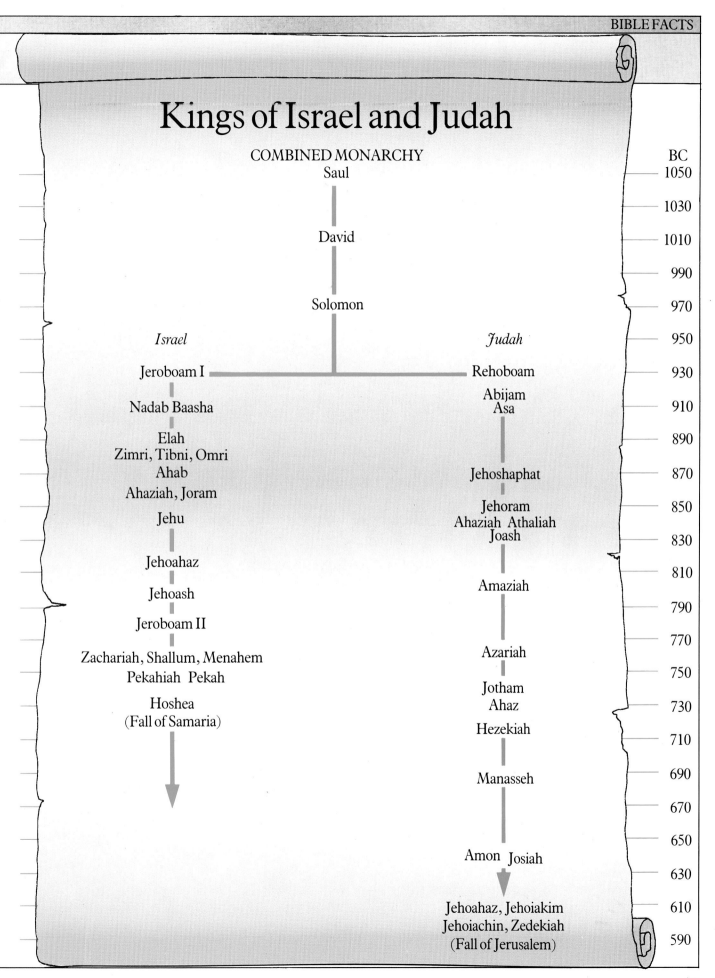

COMBINED MONARCHY
Saul

David

Solomon

Israel   *Judah*

Jeroboam I   Rehoboam

Nadab Baasha   Abijam
                                                    Asa

Elah
Zimri, Tibni, Omri
Ahab   Jehoshaphat
Ahaziah, Joram
                                                    Jehoram
Jehu   Ahaziah Athaliah
                                                    Joash

Jehoahaz

Jehoash   Amaziah

Jeroboam II

Zachariah, Shallum, Menahem   Azariah
Pekahiah Pekah
                                                    Jotham
Hoshea   Ahaz
(Fall of Samaria)
                                                    Hezekiah

                                                    Manasseh

                                                    Amon Josiah

                                                    Jehoahaz, Jehoiakim
                                                    Jehoiachin, Zedekiah
                                                    (Fall of Jerusalem)

BC
1050

1030

1010

990

970

950

930

910

890

870

850

830

810

790

770

750

730

710

690

670

650

630

610

590

37

MUSIC IN THE BIBLE

Music appears to have played an important part in Hebrew culture from the earliest times. Cain's descendant Jubal is said to be "the father of all such as handle the harp and organ" (Gen. 4:21). Music was used for all kinds of occasions, both sacred and secular.

The Bible includes accounts of music being played at feasts (e.g. Is. 5:12) and at funerals (Matt. 9:23). Music was also used to celebrate triumph in battle (Ex. 15:20–21; 2 Chron. 20:28), and was part of religious worship.

A procession of musicians found on a bowl of Phoenician make, dating from the eighth century BC

When we think of music in the Old Testament we are inevitably drawn to **David**, the shepherd boy who calmed **King Saul** with the music of his harp (1 Sam. 16:14–23) and composed the psalms and the lamentation for Saul and **Jonathan** (2 Sam. 1:17–27). David seems to have been a natural poet and musician, whose worship of God was often expressed in singing and dancing. He organized the choir and instrumentalists to accompany the ark of the covenant into **Jerusalem** (1 Chron. 15:16–24) and is said to have had four thousand instrumentalists (1 Chron. 23:5). **Solomon** seems to have taken after his father: he wrote a thousand and five songs (1 Kgs. 4:32) and organized a huge choir and orchestra to celebrate the dedication of the temple (2 Chron. 5:12–13).

MUSICAL INSTRUMENTS

We have no accurate knowledge of what the music we read of in the Bible sounded like, but we have a little more idea about the instruments used. None have survived, but we can draw some conclusions about them from musical instruments of the period that have been found in Egypt and Mesopotamia.

*King David was primarily responsible for the introduction of music into formal religious ceremony. The picture **below**, from a medieval manuscript, shows David playing his harp and surrounded by musicians*

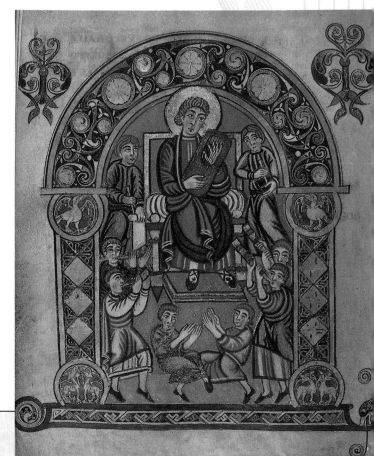

Strings

The instrument which is translated as "harp" in the King James Version is more likely to have been a lyre, for the indications are that it was a fairly small, portable instrument (1 Sam. 10:5). It was made of wood, and had eight or ten strings, which may have been plucked with a plectrum. It could have been of Syrian origin: Laban the Syrian reproaches **Jacob** for stealing away without a proper send-off "with songs … and harp" (Gen. 31:27). The popular association of harps with heaven comes from John's vision of the heavenly throne in Revelation 14:2.

The instrument which is sometimes translated as "psaltery" (2 Sam. 10:5) and sometimes "viol" (e.g. Is. 5:12) was also a kind of small wooden-framed harp, which was plucked with the fingers. It may have been of Phoenician origin.

The instruments played in **Nebuchadnezzar**'s orchestra (Dan. 3:5) have been mistranslated in the King James Version. The instrument translated as "sackbut" was in fact a kind of harp, possibly of triangular shape, whereas the instrument rendered as "dulcimer" was not a stringed instrument at all, but a kind of bagpipe.

Wind Instruments

The instrument translated as "pipe" is thought to have been something like an oboe. It was used in festivals and for rejoicing (e.g. 1 Kgs. 1:40), but also for funerals: the mournful Jeremiah compared a sad heart to the sound of pipes (Jer. 48:36).

The word "trumpet" in the King James Version refers to more than one instrument. It is used for the traditional ram's horn – the shofar still used in synagogues today – and for the silver trumpet used by **Moses** (Num. 10:1–10). The word "cornet" is also sometimes used

This picture of an Egyptian musician, playing a stringed instrument, was painted on a tomb from the reign of Thutmose IV 1420–11 BC

instead of trumpet, although the instrument referred to in 2 Samuel 6:5 as a "cornet" (King James Version) was probably some kind of percussion instrument.

"Organ" seems to be rendered as a term for wind instruments in general (e.g. Gen. 4:21; Job 21:12). The word "flute" occurs only in Daniel 3:5, and probably was something that we would recognize as a flute.

Percussion

There are two different words which are translated as "cymbals," and the different words may have referred to the two kinds of cymbal used. One kind had two flat metal plates which were clashed together; in the other they were cup-shaped and one was struck down on the other, which remained stationary. These may have been the two cymbals in Psalm 150:5. Cymbals were used at the dedication of the wall of Jerusalem (Neh. 12:27).

The "timbrel" or "tabret" was a kind of tambourine, which was used on joyous occasions, usually to accompany singing and dancing (e.g. Ex. 15:20; 1 Sam. 18:6).

CHRONICLES

Believed for many years to be the writings of the prophet Ezra, but of anonymous authorship, the two books of Chronicles were originally one, and were probably written around the fourth century BC.

The first nine chapters consist entirely of genealogies. The remainder of the books is an account of historical events which parallels accounts given in the books of Samuel and Kings. Sometimes the accounts are almost identical, but Chronicles puts a greater stress on religious ritual and on God's faithfulness to his people.

EZRA

The prophet Ezra was traditionally thought to be the author, although many now believe it to date from the third century BC.

The book gives an account of the release of a group of Jews from captivity in **Babylon**, and their return to **Jerusalem**. Much of the book is concerned with the building and dedication of the second temple, a work which is constantly hindered by the actions of hostile Persian rulers. The concluding chapters describe how Ezra traveled from Persia to Jerusalem in order to teach and enforce the law, and how he dealt with the problem of intermarriage between the Jews and alien peoples.

The longest-lived man in the Bible is Methuselah, who is said to have been 969 years old when he died (Gen. 5:27). Jared lived for 962 years (Gen. 5:20). Adam lived for 930 years (Gen. 5:5) and his son Seth for 912 (Gen. 5:8). After the Flood, there are no more such extraordinarily long lives, but the patriarchs all achieved great ages. Abraham lived to 175 (Gen. 25:7), Isaac to 180 (Gen. 35:28), Jacob to 147 (Gen. 47:28), and Joseph to 110 (Gen. 50:22). Moses died at 120 and "his eye was not dim, nor his natural force abated" (Deut. 34:7). Life expectancy apparently became shorter, for Psalm 90:10 reckons the human life span at seventy or eighty years.

NEHEMIAH

This book was originally part of the book of Ezra and was written in the same period.

The book is a first-person narrative told by the statesman and spiritual leader Nehemiah. Its content is very similar to that of the book of Ezra, with an account of the rebuilding of the walls of **Jerusalem** by Jews returned from the Babylonian captivity. Chapters eight and nine continue the account of Ezra's work in upholding the law. The book concludes with Nehemiah's reforms of various abuses in religious practice.

ESTHER

The book of Esther has been held in the past to have been written by Mordecai, one of its protagonists, but is now widely believed to have been written in the later part of the second century BC.

The book is a narrative account of the deliverance of the Jews within the Persian empire by **Esther**, a Jewish woman who had become the wife of the Persian king **Ahasuerus**. Acting on the instructions of her cousin Mordecai, Esther averted the plans of the wicked Haman, and prevented a massacre of her people. These events are celebrated annually in the Jewish festival of Purim.

JOB

Traditionally thought to be the work of **Moses**, but there are very few clues either to authorship or date. Most scholars place it around the fourth century BC.

Apart from the introductory and concluding passages, the book is written as poetry. It deals with the problem of unmerited suffering by telling the story of a blameless man called **Job**, who is subjected by God to bereavement, loss of wealth, and great physical misery, in order to test his faith. The book includes long debates between Job and his friends about the nature of suffering and its relationship to sin. In the concluding chapters God answers Job, and at the end of the book his health and wealth are restored.

For I know that my redeemer liveth, and that he shall stand at the latter day upon the earth: And though ... worms destroy this body, yet in my flesh shall I see God. (Job 19:25–26)

PSALMS

Nearly half the psalms in this book are attributed to **David**. The book appears to be a compilation of

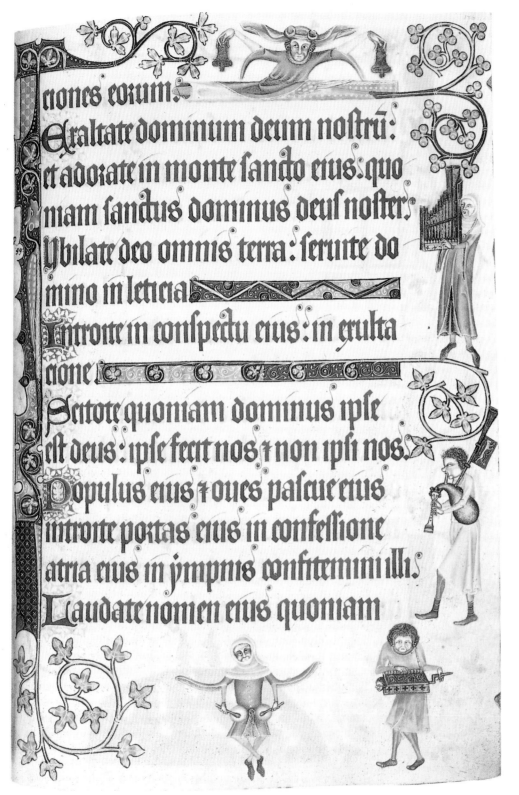

ciones eorum.

Exaltate dominum deum nostru:
et adorate in monte sancto eius. quo
niam sanctus dominus deus noster.

Ubilate deo omnis terra: seruite do
mino in leticia

Introite in conspectu eius: in exulta
cione

Scitote quoniam dominus ipse
est deus: ipse fecit nos 7 non ipsi nos.
Populus eius 7 oues pascue eius
introite portas eius in confessione
atria eius in ympnis confitemini illi.
Laudate nomen eius quoniam

The psalms have always been among the best loved parts of the Bible, and illustrated books of psalms, known as psalters, were once common. This page is from the Luttrell Psalter

A picture from an Anglo-Saxon psalter, illustrating Psalm 11, a psalm of David

INFINEM PRO OCTAVA PSAL

several collections of psalms, many written during the time of the monarchy (c. 1050–600 BC), but some after the Babylonian exile.

The psalms are essentially poems, which were intended to be set to music. The collection is often referred to as "the hymnbook of the second temple." It includes songs of praise, thanksgiving, and atonement; pleas for God's protection; and expressions of hope in a Messiah. The psalms were (and still are) used in synagogue services, and some are used for particular liturgical purposes: for example, the "songs of degrees" (or "ascents") were used as processional songs.

The Lord is my shepherd; I shall not want. He maketh me to lie down in green pastures: he leadeth me beside the still waters. He restoreth my soul: he leadeth me in the paths of righteousness for his name's sake. Yea, though I walk through the valley of the shadow of death, I will fear no evil: for thou art with me; thy rod and thy staff they comfort me. Thou preparest a table before me in the presence of mine enemies: thou anointest my head with oil; my cup runneth over. Surely goodness and mercy shall follow me all the days of my life: and I will dwell in the house of the Lord for ever. (Ps. 23)

PROVERBS

Traditionally thought to have been written in part by **Solomon**, the various parts of the book of Proverbs

DAVID · XI ·

date from different times, but would not have been put together before the fifth century BC.

The first nine chapters consist of reflections and exhortations on the nature of wisdom. The next twelve chapters present "the proverbs of Solomon," and are mainly practical instruction on the life of wisdom and

The book of books, the storehouse and magazine of life and comfort, the holy Scriptures.
GEORGE HERBERT 1593–1633

righteousness. Other "sayings of the wise" reflect on religious and social responsibilities; these are followed by further proverbs attributed to Solomon, and the unknown Agur and Lemuel, ending with a poem in praise of virtuous wives.

Go to the ant, thou sluggard; consider her ways, and be wise. (Prov. 6:6)

ECCLESIASTES

The book of Ecclesiastes is now ascribed to an unknown author writing around 200 BC, although it was believed for a long time to be the work of **Solomon**.

The author calls himself "the Preacher," and the book is a reflection on the meaning and purpose of life. He examines the nature of wisdom, pleasure, riches, and the inevitability of death. His conclusion is that "all is vanity" and our only duty is to keep God's commandments. Much of the book consists of practical observations and advice, similar to that found in the book of Proverbs.

To every thing there is a season, and a time to every purpose under the heaven: a time to be born and a time to die … a time to weep and a time to laugh; a time to mourn, and a time to dance … (Eccles. 3:1–2,4)

SONG OF SOLOMON

Although originally ascribed to **Solomon**, the book is now thought by many to have been written at a later date.

At face value this book is a collection of love poems, of a lyrical, personal, and often erotic nature. There is virtually no religious content, but the poems have often been interpreted as having allegorical significance as a portrait of God's love for his people, or of Christ's relationship with the Church.

Rise up, my love, my fair one, and come away. For, lo, the winter is past, the rain is over and gone; the flowers appear on the earth; the time of the singing of birds is come, and the voice of the turtle is heard in our land. (Song 2: 10–12)

ISAIAH

Although some of the prophecies in this book originate from Isaiah himself, the book is now widely believed to have three separate authors, the latest writing in the fifth century BC.

The first thirty-nine chapters are the oldest and it is these that are most widely credited to the prophet Isaiah, who lived in the eighth century BC. These chapters contain political and spiritual prophecy, with the author foreseeing the eventual fall of **Babylon** and Assyria, but also speaking of the kingdom of peace and the coming of the Messiah. Chapters 40–55 are prophecies of freedom from the Babylonian exile, and the restoration of Zion. The final chapters contain various prophecies, mainly of a spiritual nature. The book is valued greatly for its Messianic prophecies.

For unto us a child is born, unto us a son is given: and the government shall be upon his shoulder: and his name shall be called Wonderful, Counselor, The Mighty God, The Everlasting Father, The Prince of Peace. (Is. 9:6)

JEREMIAH

Much of the book was written by Jeremiah himself, who lived at the end of the seventh century BC, though some portions may be the work of the scribe Baruch (who acted as secretary to Jeremiah), or of later scribes.

Jeremiah's ministry was spread over forty years and five reigns, and he witnessed the fall of **Jerusalem** to **Babylon**. His personality – emotional, sensitive, melancholic – comes over more clearly than that of any other prophet, and his appeal is to the individual as much as to the nation. The messages of the book are the condemnation of idolatry and immorality, lamentations for the sins of the people and a call to repentance, and prophecies of judgment and of the eventual redemption of Israel.

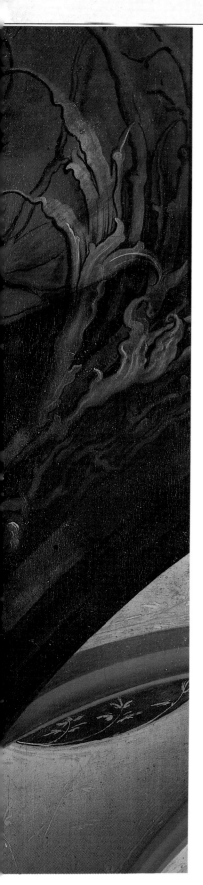

Far left A fifteenth-century German representation of the prophet Isaiah

Left The Prophet Isaiah by Grünewald (c. 1470-1528), from the Isenheim Altarpiece

Below The Vision of Ezekiel by Francisco Collantes (1599–1656). The picture illustrates Ezekiel's vision of the valley of dry bones (Ezek. 37)

LAMENTATIONS

Believed originally to have been written by Jeremiah, Lamentations is now usually thought to be the work of more than one author. None of it is likely to date from later than the end of the sixth century BC.

The first four chapters are acrostic poems, written to a formal pattern, and the final chapter is similar in form to some of the psalms. The content is a dirge-like lament for the fall of **Jerusalem**, comparing its past glories with its present desolation, and interpreting the fall as God's punishment for sin.

It is of the Lord's mercies that we are not consumed, because his compassions fail not. They are new every morning: great is thy faithfulness. (Lam. 3:22–23)

EZEKIEL

Many believe at least most of the book to be the work of Ezekiel himself, and thus dating from the end of the sixth century BC.

Ezekiel was one of those deported to **Babylon** and he is writing for the Jews in captivity. Apart from the

FOOD AND DRINK IN THE BIBLE

Food and drink play an important part in many Bible stories. Fasting and feasting have always been essential elements of Judaism, and the central Christian sacrament is based on the fellowship meal. The following is an account of the main foods eaten in Bible times.

CEREAL FOODS

Cereal crops have always provided the staple diet. Many of the Bible references do not specify the particular variety of cereal, but speak generally of "grain" or "corn" (e.g. Gen. 42:2). Both in Old and New Testament times, wheat was valued more highly than barley (Rev. 6:6); barley flour was generally used by poorer people (John 6:9). Millet was also grown, as well as an inferior kind of wheat called spelt ("rie" in the King James Version; e.g. Ex. 9:32).

VEGETABLES

The Israelites in the wilderness remembered with nostalgia the cucumbers, leeks, onion, and garlic that they had eaten in Egypt (Num. 11:5). The vegetables available in Palestine were probably more limited, although lentils and beans were common (Gen. 25:34; 2 Sam. 17:28).

DAIRY FOODS

Milk was drunk from the earliest times, when the semi-nomadic tribes lived on the dairy products of their flocks. Although it was a staple, it was highly valued ("a land flowing with milk and honey") and also offered to guests (Judg. 4:19). Milk was churned to make butter (Prov. 30:33) and the curds were used for cheese (1 Sam. 17:18; Job 10:10).

FRUIT

The most important fruits were probably olives, which provided oil, and grapes, which were eaten fresh or dried as raisins (Deut. 23:24; 1 Sam. 25:18), besides being made into wine. Figs were popular as food and for medicinal use (Is. 38:21). Pomegranates were valued for their juice (Song 8:2) and apples were probably grown (Song 2:5). Nuts included almonds and pistachios (Gen. 43:11).

MEAT AND FISH

Meat was not a staple. It was eaten on special occasions and offered to honored guests. The fatted calf was offered to **Abraham**'s angelic visitors (Gen. 18:6) as well as to the

Prodigal Son (Luke 15:23). In early Old Testament days, game was hunted for food (Gen. 27:3–4), but by New Testament times, the dietary laws were strictly enforced, and only properly slaughtered animals were eaten. Fish, too, were subject to the dietary laws, but were apparently eaten more frequently than meat. The Gospels abound with accounts of fishing and the resurrected Jesus ate fish with his disciples (Luke 24:42–43; John 21:9–13).

SEASONING AND COOKING

Honey was a much prized delicacy (Ps. 19:10). It was the only form of sweetening and was probably only available to richer people. It was used in cooking to make cakes (Ex. 16:31), although normally "cakes" in the Bible refers to flat loaves of meal, water, and salt (e.g. Gen. 18:6). Herbs and spices used in cooking included dill ("anise" in the King James Version), coriander, mint, cumin, and rue (Num. 11:7; Is. 28:25; Matt. 23:23; Luke 11:42), although the main seasoning was always salt (Job 6:6). Cooking in Egypt was probably more sophisticated, at least for rich people. The baker who was **Joseph**'s fellow-prisoner made all kinds of baked goods for Pharaoh (Gen. 40:16–17).

ALCOHOL

The most common alcoholic drink was wine, made from grapes, which is mentioned many times in both Old and New Testaments. Jesus drank wine with his friends and changed water into wine at **Cana** (Matt. 11:19; John 2:1–10), and **Paul** recommended wine to **Timothy** for its medicinal properties (1 Tim. 5:23). In Egypt and Mesopotamia, beer brewed from grain was also popular, and a kind of wine was made from dates.

JEWISH DIETARY LAWS

The dietary laws which were followed by Jews in Bible times, and are still adhered to by orthodox Jews today, are mainly concentrated in Leviticus 11 and Deuteronomy 14. Animals that were forbidden as food included pigs, rabbits, camels, and any animal that had been killed violently or died of natural causes (Lev. 17:15). Birds of prey were forbidden as food, and so were shellfish.

Eating the blood of animals was forbidden even before the law was given to Moses (Gen. 9:4). Part of the ritual of making meat *kosher* involves draining all blood from the slaughtered animal.

The prohibition on eating milk products at the same time as meat derives from the edict "Thou shalt not seethe a kid in its mother's milk" (Ex. 23:19). This is thought to refer to idolatrous sacrificial practices which were rife in **Canaan** at the time.

Special rules apply to the feast of Passover. Besides eating the ritual meal of lamb and bitter herbs, unleavened bread must be eaten for a week and no leavened food is allowed in the house (Ex. 12:1–20).

Most Jewish feast days have special food associated with them, and this is specially true of the Passover, where a ritual meal is eaten, and no leavened food is allowed for seven days. This illustration from a medieval Jewish manuscript, The Golden Haggadah, tells the story of the institution of the Passover

message of judgment and the need for repentance, the book of Ezekiel is marked by its emphasis on ritual and its descriptions of the prophet's visions. These include the vision of the valley of dry bones which God brings to life.

DANIEL

Traditionally held to be the work of **Daniel** himself, the book is now generally believed to have been written by an unknown author at a much later date, possibly as late as the middle of the second century BC.

The first six chapters are a narrative account of how Daniel and his friends were taken as captives from **Judah** to **Babylon**, how they grew in wisdom and remained faithful to God. These chapters include the familiar stories of Daniel's interpretation of **Nebuchadnezzar**'s dreams, the fiery furnace, **Belshazzar**'s feast, and Daniel's deliverance from the lions' den. The second half of the book is an account of Daniel's prophetic visions. These mystical prophecies have been the subject of many attempts at interpretation, particularly those relating them to the Antichrist and the Second Coming.

HOSEA

The book appears to originate from the prophet Hosea himself and to date from the end of the eighth century BC.

The prophet describes how God instructs him to marry the whorish Gomer and how he remains faithful to her despite her desertion and adultery. This is used as an allegorical picture of God's relationship with a sinful and idolatrous Israel. Hosea reproves Israel for its sins and exhorts the people to repent.

JOEL

It is not known when the prophet Joel lived and the book is very difficult to date, although it is now thought probably to have been written in the fourth century BC.

The book begins with an account of the destruction wrought by a great plague of locusts and a prophesy of

Left Daniel's vision of the four beasts and God enthroned, from a Mozarabic Bible of 1109. The vision is described in Daniel 7

The king who had the longest reign mentioned in the Bible was Manasseh, who reigned as king of Judah for fifty-five years (2 Kgs 21:1). The shortest reign was that of Zimri, who was king of Israel for only seven days (1 Kgs. 16:15).

how God will bless and restore the land when the people repent. Joel then prophesies about the gifts of the Spirit and the last days. The third and last chapter speaks of God's judgment on the nations.

And it shall come to pass afterward, that I will pour out my spirit upon all flesh; and your sons and your daughters shall prophesy, your old men shall dream dreams, your young men shall see visions. (Joel 2:28)

AMOS

Much of the book probably originates from the eighth-century prophet Amos himself, although it is likely that other authors were involved and the final compilation may have taken place at a later date.

The first section concerns God's judgment on the Gentile nations; Amos next turns to the sins of Israel and calls on the people to repent. The prophet then describes five different visions that God has sent him, each symbolizing judgment. The book ends with a promise of restoration. Amos' message is notable for its stress on righteousness, in both a spiritual and a social context. He denounces the empty religious ritual of his day, and in strong terms condemns the oppression of the poor by the wealthy.

But let judgment run down as waters, and righteousness as a mighty stream. (Amos 5:24)

OBADIAH

This is the shortest book of the Old Testament. It is not clear when the prophet Obadiah lived but many believe the work to date from the fifth century BC.

The twenty-one verses of the book are a denunciation of Edom and a prophecy of its doom and destruction, finishing with a prophecy of the restoration of Zion.

Prosperity is the blessing of the Old Testament, adversity is the blessing of the New.
FRANCIS BACON 1561–1626

JONAH

Both date and authorship are uncertain, but the book is thought to have been written in the sixth century BC or possibly later.

The first chapter relates how the prophet **Jonah** is told by God to go to the city of **Nineveh** to denounce the sinfulness of its people. Jonah rebels against God and takes a ship bound in the opposite direction. He is thrown overboard and swallowed by a large fish. The next chapter is Jonah's prayer to God from the fish's belly. Jonah is delivered onto dry land and chapter 3 tells of how God again commands him to go to Nineveh. This time Jonah obeys and predicts the fall of the city. The people repent; a fast is proclaimed and even the king dons sackcloth and ashes. Because of their repentance God reprieves them from punishment.

The final chapter describes Jonah's anger at Nineveh's escape from judgment. He shelters under a gourd which God then destroys, showing Jonah that, as he regrets the loss of the gourd, God would pity the loss of so many human beings.

MICAH

The book of Micah is traditionally believed to be the work of the prophet Micah, a younger contemporary of Isaiah, but it is widely thought that the last part of the book belongs to a later period.

Micah begins with a prophecy of judgment on Israel and a condemnation of oppressive rulers and corrupt priests. He goes on to prophesy a time of peace and righteousness, when Zion would be glorious again, and foresees the coming of a Messiah from **Bethlehem**. The book continues with a reiteration of the message against corruption in religion and society, but closes with praise for God's mercy.

… and they shall beat their swords into plowshares, and their spears into pruninghooks: nation shall not lift up a sword against nation, neither shall they learn war any more. But they shall sit every man under his vine and under his fig tree; and none shall make them afraid . (Mic. 4:3–4)

Jonah was swallowed by "a great fish," often interpreted as being a whale, although the creature in this engraving seems to be a wholly imaginary sea monster

WORDS AND PHRASES FROM THE BIBLE

There are many common words and phrases in the English language which came originally from the Bible, although their users do not always realize their derivation.

The Good Samaritan *by Luca Giordano (1632–1705). The familiar phrase comes from the parable Jesus tells in Luke 10, which demonstrates that whoever treats a needy person with compassion is that person's neighbor*

WORDS AND PHRASES TAKEN FROM PROPER NAMES

Some of these are a direct reference to the personality of a Bible character. Thus, wicked women are called Jezebels or Delilahs, pessimists are called Jeremiahs, traitors are Judases, doubters are doubting Thomases, and those who depress friends who need consolation are Job's comforters. A Jonah is someone who is thought to bring bad luck. To raise cain, meaning to behave in a wild manner, probably derives from Cain's violent nature. It is less obvious why a jeroboam, a wine bottle holding just over three liters, is named after two kings of Israel.

Other words derive from Bible places. A babel, meaning a scene of noise and confusion, comes from the place name Babel, where God created a confusion of languages (Gen. 11:1–9). Sodomy and sodomite refer to the ancient city of Sodom, whose men were noted for their homosexual lust (Gen. 19:1–11).

SOME PHRASES FROM THE OLD TESTAMENT

The fat of the land (Gen. 45:18)
By the skin of one's teeth (Job. 19:20)
Pride goes before a fall (Prov. 16:18)
Nothing new under the sun (Eccles. 1:8)
Eat, drink, and be merry (Eccles. 8:15)
A fly in the ointment (Eccles. 10:1)
Woe is me! (Is. 6:5)
A drop in a bucket (Is. 40:15)
Like a lamb to the slaughter (Is. 53:7)
Holier than thou (Is. 65:5)
A leopard cannot change its spots (Jer. 13:23)

SOME PHRASES FROM THE NEW TESTAMENT

The salt of the earth (Matt. 5:13)
Pearls before swine (Matt. 7:6)
The straight and narrow (Matt. 7:14)
A wolf in sheep's clothing (Matt. 7:15)
The blind leading the blind (Matt. 15:14)
A good samaritan (Luke 10:30–37)
No respecter of persons (Acts 10:34–35)
The powers that be (Rom. 13:1)
All things to all men (1 Cor. 9:22)
A thorn in the flesh (2 Cor. 12:7)

NAHUM

The book appears to have been written by the prophet Nahum in the later part of the seventh century BC.

Nahum's message is a prophecy of the doom of the city of **Nineveh**. The first chapter is in the form of an acrostic poem praising God for his goodness and mercy, but stressing his great power and his ability to overthrow the wicked. The second chapter describes how Nineveh will be attacked and despoiled, and the final chapter tells of the wickedness of Nineveh, comparing it with Thebes (Hebrew *No*), a once great city that fell to the Assyrians.

HABAKKUK

Little is known about the prophet Habakkuk, and both date and authorship of the book are uncertain, although it is widely thought to date from the end of the seventh century BC.

At the beginning of the book the prophet cries to God for failing to punish wickedness and injustice. God tells him that he is raising up the ruthless Chaldeans to overthrow the land, but Habakkuk protests that the Chaldeans are brutal and idolatrous, and so cannot be used by God to execute his judgment. In the second chapter God answers Habakkuk by telling him that the Chaldeans will be judged for their pride and violence, while faithfulness and righteousness will be rewarded. The third chapter is a psalm about God's judgment and salvation.

ZEPHANIAH

Zephaniah is thought to have been a contemporary of Nahum and Jeremiah, and the book was probably written in the late seventh century BC.

It is an apocalyptic work, prophesying the "day of the Lord." The first chapter prophesies doom and destruction on **Judah** and **Jerusalem**, while the second prophesies God's judgment on various foreign nations. The final chapter reverts once more to the judgment of Jerusalem, reproving the city for its sins, but promising blessing for the faithful remnant.

HAGGAI

The book contains messages of the prophet Haggai, which were delivered during three months in the year 520 BC.

*The restoration of the Temple in Jerusalem was the most urgent task facing the Jewish people after the Babylonian captivity. These two illustrations from a Bible dictionary of 1732 show (**left**) Solomon dedicating his temple to the Lord and, (**above right**) the temple and surrounding buildings*

The prophet was writing after the return from captivity in **Babylon**. Work on the rebuilding of the temple had stopped, and Haggai's task was to urge the people to return to this work. He reproves them for their lethargy and they begin the rebuilding again, with the cooperation of the governor Zerubbabel. Haggai delivers God's message that the temple will be restored to its former glories, and the book ends with a Messianic prophecy.

ZECHARIAH

The first eight chapters are assumed to originate with the prophet Zechariah, and date from the late sixth century BC, while the latter part of the book appears to belong to a much later period.

The first part of the book dates from the time of the rebuilding of the temple. The prophet describes a series of visions of a Messianic nature, describing a new Jerusalem and the restoration of Zion. Chapters 9–14 are also concerned with Messianic prophecy. They include predictions of the coming of a just but lowly king, the raising up of a good shepherd, and the mourning of **Jerusalem** for the one "whom they have pierced."

Rejoice greatly, O Daughter of Zion; shout, O daughter of Jerusalem: behold, thy King cometh unto thee: he is just, and having salvation; lowly, and riding upon an ass, and upon a colt the foal of an ass. (Zech. 9:9)

MALACHI

It is not certain whether Malachi is the proper name of an actual prophet or is a common noun meaning "my messenger," but the book is thought to have been written in the fifth century BC.

The first two chapters declare God's love for Israel and a description of the people's sins. The attack is directed particularly against the priests, who were offering polluted sacrifices. The second half of the book is concerned with God's judgment and blessings. It speaks of the coming day of the Lord, reproves the people for withholding tithes, and promises deliverance for the righteous.

Books of the New Testament

NARRATIVE
Matthew
Mark
Luke
John
Acts

LETTERS – (1) ATTRIBUTED TO PAUL
Romans
1 and 2 Corinthians
Galatians
Ephesians
Philippians
Colossians
1 and 2 Thessalonians
1 and 2 Timothy
Titus
Philemon

LETTERS – (2) DOUBTFUL OR ATTRIBUTED TO OTHER WRITERS
Hebrews
James
1 and 2 Peter
1, 2 and 3 John
Jude

VISIONARY APOCALYPTIC WRITING
Revelations

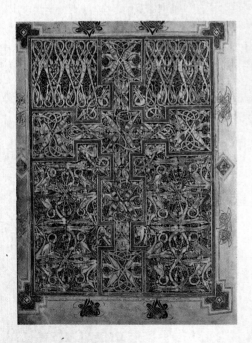

Top *The cover of the Sion Gospels, which date from AD 1000*
Left *A page from the eighth-century Lichfield Gospels*

Above *These richly-illustrated pages come from a thirteenth-century Armenian Book of Gospels, now in Jerusalem*

The Chronology of the New Testament

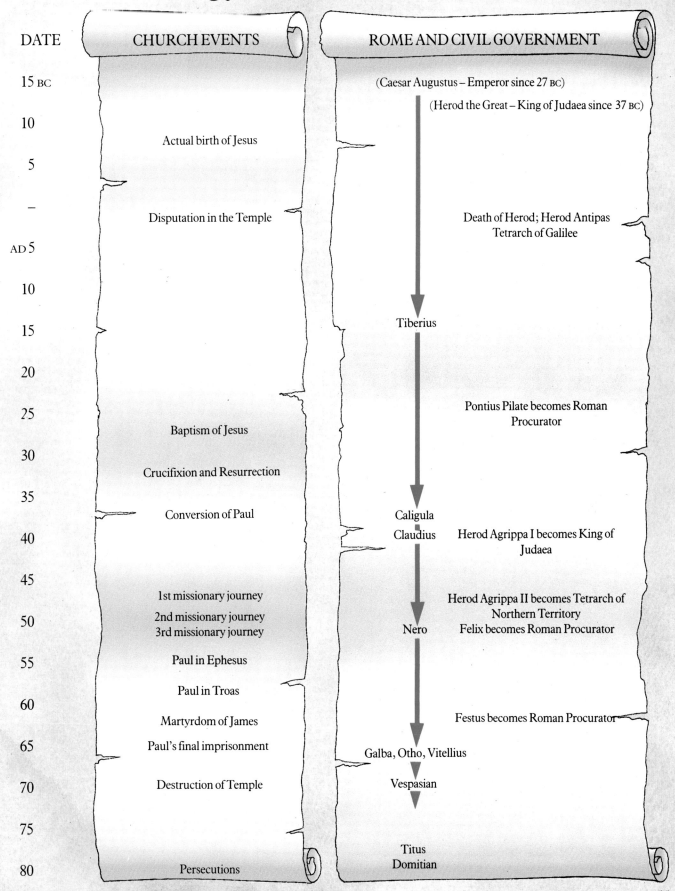

DATE	CHURCH EVENTS	ROME AND CIVIL GOVERNMENT
15 BC		(Caesar Augustus – Emperor since 27 BC)
10		(Herod the Great – King of Judaea since 37 BC)
	Actual birth of Jesus	
5		
–	Disputation in the Temple	Death of Herod; Herod Antipas Tetrarch of Galilee
AD 5		
10		
15		Tiberius
20		
25		Pontius Pilate becomes Roman Procurator
	Baptism of Jesus	
30	Crucifixion and Resurrection	
35		
	Conversion of Paul	Caligula
40		Claudius Herod Agrippa I becomes King of Judaea
45		
	1st missionary journey	Herod Agrippa II becomes Tetrarch of Northern Territory
50	2nd missionary journey 3rd missionary journey	Nero Felix becomes Roman Procurator
55	Paul in Ephesus	
	Paul in Troas	
60	Martyrdom of James	Festus becomes Roman Procurator
65	Paul's final imprisonment	Galba, Otho, Vitellius
70	Destruction of Temple	Vespasian
75		
80	Persecutions	Titus Domitian

GOSPEL OF MATTHEW

Traditionally thought to have been written by the apostle **Matthew**, the book is now believed to be of unknown authorship and to date from about AD 85–90.

This is one of the three "synoptic Gospels" (Matthew, Mark, Luke), which give a broad view of the life of Jesus, and there is considerable overlap in the content. The Gospel appears to have been written specifically for a Jewish audience. It contains many references to Old Testament prophecies about the Messiah, and there is an attempt to trace Jesus' genealogy back to **Abraham**. There is also an emphasis on Jesus' ethical teaching, which is presented as a fulfillment of the Jewish law. Matthew's Gospel contains a number of parables not found elsewhere and in several of these the theme is the kingdom of heaven, with emphasis on judgment and eternal punishment for the wicked.

Blessed are the poor in spirit: for theirs is the kingdom of heaven. Blessed are they that mourn: for they shall be comforted. Blessed are the meek: for they shall inherit the earth. Blessed are they which do hunger and thirst after righteousness: for they shall be filled. Blessed are the merciful: for they shall obtain mercy. Blessed are the pure in heart: for they shall see God. Blessed are the peacemakers: for they shall be called the children of God. (Matt. 5:3–9)

GOSPEL OF MARK

Usually thought to have been written by **Mark** of **Jerusalem**, the companion of **Paul**, **Peter**, and **Barnabas**, this is generally assumed to be the earliest of the four Gospels, written between AD 65 and 70.

Mark's Gospel is a simple, straightforward account of Jesus' life, and is the source for much of Matthew's and Luke's Gospels. The book appears to have been written for Gentiles, for there is little reference to the Old Testament. Mark's Gospel begins with the baptism of Jesus by **John the Baptist**; there is no account of his birth or his life before his ministry began. The book ends abruptly with the resurrected Jesus appearing to the women at the tomb. The last twelve verses of Chapter 16 are thought to be a later addition.

Suffer the little children to come unto me, and forbid them not: for of such is the kingdom of God. (Mark 10:14)

GOSPEL OF LUKE

Almost certainly written by the physician and companion of **Paul**, Luke's Gospel is of uncertain date, but it was probably written in the last quarter of the first century AD.

The last of the synoptic Gospels to be written, Luke's Gospel uses both Matthew and Mark for source material. Like Mark, Luke was writing for Gentiles: Jesus' genealogy is traced back to **Adam** rather than

Left Altar panels showing Christ and Four Saints by Edward Burne-Jones (1833–1896). The saints represented are apparently the four evangelists, Matthew, Mark, Luke, and John

Above The crucifixion of Christ has been taken as a subject by many artists. This modern version is by Graham Sutherland (1903–1980)

Abraham, and Luke speaks of Jesus' dealings with Gentiles and Samaritans. He gives us the fullest account of the birth and early life of Jesus. This is the most literary of the Gospels; people and events are finely observed. It is also the Gospel that emphasizes most the humanitarian aspects of Jesus' ministry: his concern for sinners and outcasts, the poor, the sick, and women.

Fear not: for, behold, I bring you tidings of great joy, which shall be to all people. For unto you is born this day in the city of David a Savior, which is Christ the Lord. And this shall be a sign unto you; Ye shall find the babe wrapped in swaddling clothes, lying in a manger. And suddenly there was with the angel a multitude of the heavenly host praising God, and saying, Glory to God in the highest, and on earth peace, goodwill toward men. (Luke 2:10–14)

GOSPEL OF JOHN

Although it was believed to have been written by the apostle **John**, the Gospel is now thought to be of unknown authorship; it may have been partly dictated

Above A triptych illustrating scenes from the passion of Christ

***Right** The Roman empire in New Testament times*

by the apostle to an associate. It is thought to date from between AD 90 and 110.

The Gospel differs from the other three in many ways. It is less an account of Jesus' life and ministry than an attempt to interpret these events spiritually, revealing Jesus as the Messiah and Son of God. There are no parables but much figurative language, where Jesus is described as "the Word," "the light of the world," "the bread of life," "the way, the truth, and the life." Jesus' discourses in John's Gospels are longer

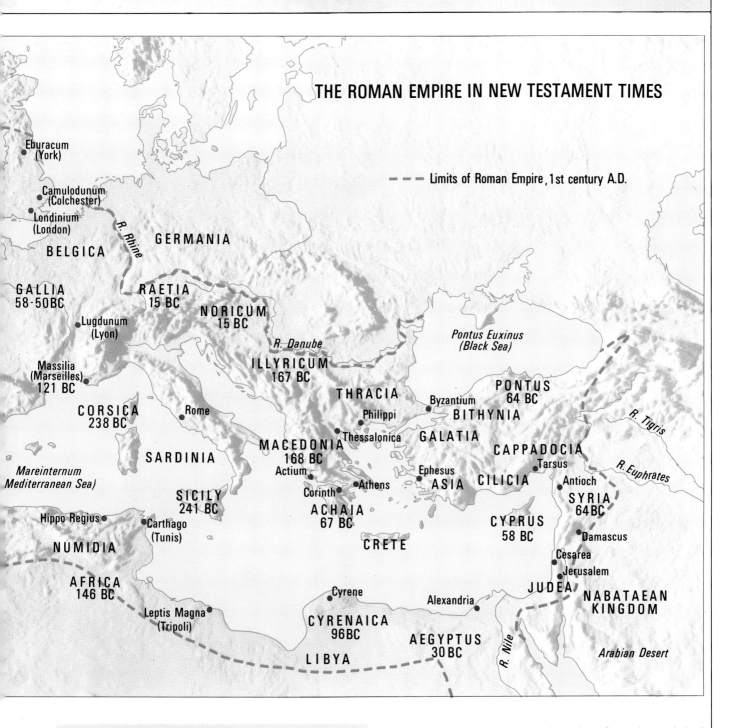

THE ROMAN EMPIRE IN NEW TESTAMENT TIMES

– – – Limits of Roman Empire, 1st century A.D.

Eburacum (York)

Camulodunum (Colchester)

Londinium (London)

BELGICA

R. Rhine

GERMANIA

GALLIA 58-50BC

RAETIA 15 BC

NORICUM 15 BC

Lugdunum (Lyon)

Massilia (Marseilles) 121 BC

R. Danube

ILLYRICUM 167 BC

Pontus Euxinus (Black Sea)

CORSICA 238 BC

Rome

THRACIA

Byzantium

Philippi

BITHYNIA

PONTUS 64 BC

R. Tigris

SARDINIA

MACEDONIA 168 BC

Thessalonica

GALATIA

CAPPADOCIA

Tarsus

R. Euphrates

Mareinternum Mediterranean Sea)

Actium

Ephesus

ASIA

CILICIA

Antioch

SICILY 241 BC

Corinth

Athens

ACHAIA 67 BC

SYRIA 64BC

Hippo Regius

Carthago (Tunis)

CRETE

CYPRUS 58 BC

Damascus

NUMIDIA

Cesarea

Jerusalem

AFRICA 146 BC

Cyrene

Alexandria

JUDEA

NABATAEAN KINGDOM

Leptis Magna (Tripoli)

CYRENAICA 96BC

AEGYPTUS 30 BC

R. Nile

Arabian Desert

LIBYA

Most people are bothered by those passages in scripture which they cannot understand; but as for me ... the passages which trouble me most are those that I do understand.
MARK TWAIN 1835–1910

and more abstract than in the other Gospels, and deal more with his relationship with his Father. Although the emphasis is not on narrative, there are some incidents recorded in John which are not in the synoptic Gospels: for example, the miracle at **Cana** and the raising of **Lazarus**.

For God so loved the world, that he gave his only begotten Son, that whosoever believeth in him should not perish, but have everlasting life. (John 3:16)

NAMES AND TITLES OF GOD AND JESUS

NAMES AND TITLES OF GOD

The Hebrew word usually translated as "God" is *elohim*, from the word *el*, which is used for gods of all kinds. Also derived from this word is the title *el elyon*, meaning "the most high God" (e.g. Gen. 14:18).

The only actual personal name of God is the Hebrew *Yahweh*, translated in English versions as "the Lord" or "Jehovah" (e.g. Gen. 12:8; Ex. 6:3). When he declared himself to Moses as "I am" (Hebrew *'ehyeh*) this can be seen as a play on the word Yahweh.

Most of God's other titles or descriptions combine the word *el* or the name Yahweh with another word. They include: "Almighty God" (e.g. Gen. 17:1), "Lord God of Israel" (e.g. Josh. 24:2), and "the Lord of hosts" (e.g. 1 Sam. 17:45). Some titles were given on one particular occasion, for example, *Jehovah-jireh* ("the Lord provides" – Gen. 23:14), *Jehovah-nissi* ("the Lord is my banner" – Ex. 17:15) and *Jehovah-shalom* ("the Lord is peace" – Judg. 6:24).

Other Old Testament names include "the Holy One of Israel" (e.g. Is. 1:4) and "the Ancient of

IoHA · 10

Days" (Dan. 7:9). Titles that are descriptions rather than names are: "Creator" (Is. 40:28), "Father" (Mal. 2:8), and "King" (e.g. Jer. 10:7). New Testament titles and descriptions, other than God and Father, are "Father of lights" (Jas. 1:17), and "King of kings and Lord of lords" (1 Tim. 6:15).

NAMES AND TITLES OF JESUS

The name Jesus is the Greek form of Joshua, which means "God is salvation"; Savior became one of his titles (e.g. Titus 1:4). Christ is the Greek form of Messiah, which means "anointed."

Before his birth Jesus was named by Isaiah as "Wonderful, Counselor, the Mighty God, the Everlasting Father, the Prince of Peace" (Is. 9:6). Isaiah also used the name Immanuel (Is. 7:14, Matt. 1:23), meaning "God with us."

Jesus often referred to himself as "the Son of man" (e.g. Matt. 8:20), but he did not deny that he was the "Son of God" (Matt. 26:63–64). Many of his most striking titles are found in John's Gospel: "the word" (1:1), "the lamb of God" (1:29), "the bread of life" (6:35), "the light of the world" (8:12), "the door" (10:9), "the good shepherd" (10:11), "the resurrection and the life" (11:25), "the way, the truth, and the life" (14:6), "the vine" (15:5). In Revelation he is called "Alpha and Omega" (1:8), "Lord of lords and King of kings" (17:14).

Left The Month of May, with Christ as the Good Shepherd *by Abel Grimmer (1570– c. 1619)*

Above The Light of the World *by William Holman Hunt (1827–1910)*

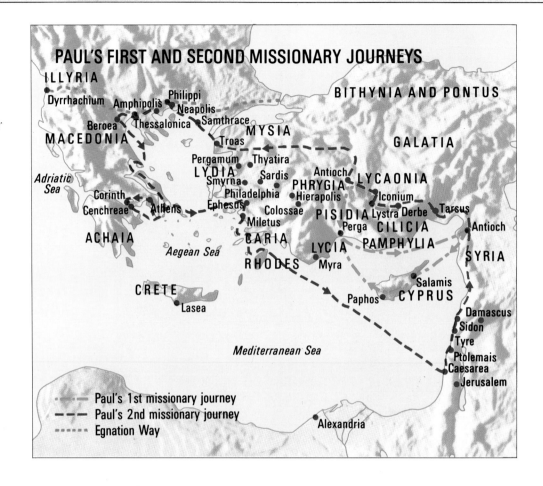

The route of Paul's first and second missionary journeys, which took him through the Roman Empire and Asia Minor

PAUL'S FIRST AND SECOND MISSIONARY JOURNEYS

- ---- Paul's 1st missionary journey
- --- Paul's 2nd missionary journey
- ••••• Egnation Way

ACTS

The Acts of the Apostles almost certainly has the same author as the Gospel of Luke and was probably written at the same period.

Acts takes up the narrative from where Luke's Gospel ends. Its style is similar to that of Luke's Gospel and there is the same humanitarian interest. The book covers a period of some thirty-three years, from Jesus' Ascension to Paul's imprisonment in Rome. The history of the early Church is told with great detail and accuracy. The main events are: the coming of the Holy Spirit and the rise of the Church at **Jerusalem**; the martyrdom of **Stephen**; the conversion of **Paul**; **Peter**'s evangelization of the Gentiles; the ministry and missionary journeys of Paul.

LETTER TO THE ROMANS

This is a letter written by the apostle **Paul** to the Roman Christians around AD 56–59.

Most of Paul's letters seem to have been written as ordinary correspondence, but this letter appears to have the primary purpose of expounding the theology of Christianity. The main themes of the book are God's righteousness and human guilt and sin. The law cannot save people from sin; this is achieved only through faith in Jesus Christ. Paul speaks of the rejection of Israel, but stresses that the gospel is for both Jews and Gentiles. Christians are called to live a life of holiness, and there is some practical advice in the concluding chapters as to how they should go about this.

For the wages of sin is death; but the gift of God is eternal life through Jesus Christ our Lord. (Rom. 6:23)

Apart from Jesus, the man mentioned most often in the Bible is David, with 1118 references, followed by Moses with 740 mentions. The woman most mentioned is Sarah with 56 references.

*A wooden carving from the Isenheim altarpiece showing the saints Paul,
Matthew, and Thomas, by Nicolas de Haguengeau (1445–1526)*

LETTERS TO THE CORINTHIANS

These two letters were written by **Paul** to the Church in **Corinth** between about AD 53 and 57.

Corinth was a town traditionally renowned for its immorality, and many of the new believers there were former pagans. Many errors and wrong practices had already arisen and Paul was writing mainly in order to correct these. In the first book he attempts to sort out problems that had arisen over Church leadership and a specific case of sexual immorality. Paul goes on to discuss questions relating to marriage, food, and worship, including how to conduct the Lord's Supper. He then speaks of spiritual gifts, praising charity (or love) as the greatest of these. The closing chapters concern the resurrection of the dead. In the second book Paul speaks at length of his personal circumstances and feelings, urges the Corinthians to holiness and liberality, and warns them against false apostles.

Paul's third missionary journey, during which he wrote the Letters to the Corinthians, the Romans and possibly the Galatians

Though I speak with the tongues of men and of angels, and have not charity, I am become as sounding brass, or a tinkling cymbal. (1 Cor. 13:1)

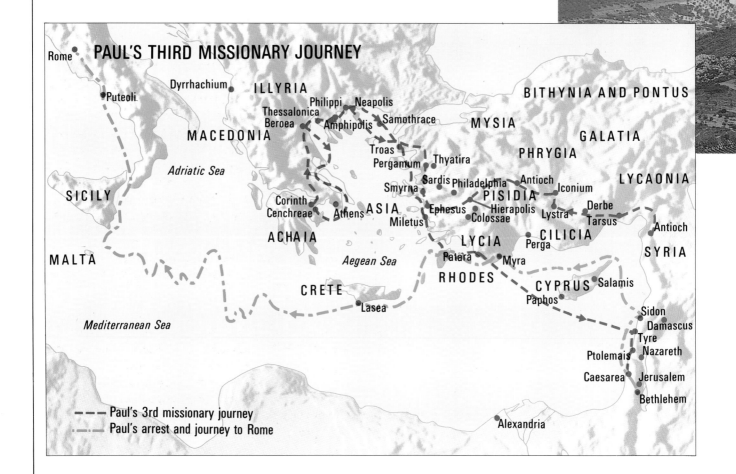

PAUL'S THIRD MISSIONARY JOURNEY

Rome
Puteoli
Dyrrhachium
ILLYRIA
BITHYNIA AND PONTUS
Philippi Neapolis
Thessalonica
Beroea Amphipolis Samothrace
MYSIA
MACEDONIA
GALATIA
Troas
PHRYGIA
Pergamum Thyatira
Adriatic Sea
LYCAONIA
Sardis Philadelphia Antioch
Iconium
SICILY
Smyrna PISIDIA
Corinth
Ephesus Hierapolis Lystra Derbe
Cenchreae Athens ASIA
Colossae Tarsus
Miletus
Antioch
ACHAIA
LYCIA Perga CILICIA
SYRIA
Aegean Sea
Patara Myra
RHODES
MALTA
CYPRUS Salamis
CRETE
Paphos
Lasea
Sidon
Mediterranean Sea
Damascus
Tyre
Ptolemais Nazareth
Caesarea Jerusalem
Bethlehem
– – – Paul's 3rd missionary journey
· – · – Paul's arrest and journey to Rome
Alexandria

Corinth, looking south-west into the Peloponnese from the acropolis of ancient Corinth

LETTER TO THE GALATIANS

This letter was written by **Paul** to the various churches of Galatia in about AD 52–56.

The Galatian Christians had apparently been led astray by those who taught that Christians must keep to the Jewish law, and Paul was writing to reestablish his authority and correct these errors. Paul reminds the Galatians that they are saved by faith, not by the works of the law, and speaks of the liberty of the Gospel that frees them from the bondage of the law. He urges them to use this liberty to serve each other in love, walking in the Spirit.

But the fruit of the Spirit is love, joy, peace, longsuffering, gentleness, goodness, faith, meekness, temperance: against such there is no law. (Gal. 5:22–23)

The Roman province of Galatia in the north of Asia Minor, where Paul founded a church

65

FLOWERS, PLANTS, AND TREES IN THE BIBLE

As with Bible fauna, the area of Bible flora is liable to give rise to misunderstandings. Translations of words for trees and plants are often inaccurate. We cannot assume that a species mentioned is the same as the species that we know under the same name, and neither can we be sure that the trees and plants growing in Bible lands now are identical to those which grew in biblical times. A selection of the many plants and trees mentioned in the scriptures are discussed below.

FLOWERS AND PLANTS

Castor Oil Plant

Castor Oil Plant
This rapidly growing plant, which withers upon handling, is thought by many to have been the "gourd" of Jonah 4, although others believe that the plant referred to was a bottle-gourd.

Hyssop
The plant known today as hyssop is native to southern Europe, so cannot be the hyssop that was used for purification rituals by the Hebrews (e.g. Ex. 12:22; Ps. 51:7). It is thought that the plant referred to was the fragrant Syrian marjoram. The "hyssop" used at the Crucifixion (John 19:29) was probably some kind of reed.

Lily
Although the word "lily" is often used in the Bible, a variety of different flowers are probably meant. The "lily of the valley" in the Song of Solomon is not the flower we know, but probably a hyacinth, although the lily that the beloved's lips are compared with (Song 5:13) is more likely to have been a red poppy anemone or scarlet tulip. The "lily-work" decorating the temple (1 Kgs. 7:19) was probably carved water-lilies. The "lilies of the field" (Matt. 6:28) could be any of many flowers – perhaps the poppy anemone or the crown marguerite.

Mandrake
A flowering herb of the nightshade family. It bears fragrant fruit in the spring (Song 7:13). It is said to have medicinal qualities and was also valued for its aphrodisiac properties and power to promote conception – attributes which **Leah** and **Rachel** obviously knew about (Gen. 30:14–16).

Myrtle

Myrtle

A common shrub of the Palestinian hillside, with fragrant leaves and flowers. Isaiah used it as a symbol of God's generosity (41:19, 55:13) and Zechariah saw myrtle trees in a vision (1:8–11). Myrtle branches were used to make booths for the festival of Tabernacles (Neh. 8:16).

Rose

The translation "rose" is used several times in the apocryphal books of the Bible, and "rose of Sharon" in the Song of Solomon (2:1). The true rose is, however, unusual in Israel, and unlikely to have been intended. The rose of Sharon is thought to have been the anemone, crocus, or narcissus.

Wormwood

Wormwood

Many species of this plant grow in Palestine. All have a peculiarly bitter taste, and the word is always used to symbolize bitterness, sorrow, and disaster (e.g. Prov. 5:4; Amos 5:7).

Mandrake

Almond

The almond tree was valued for its oil and nuts (Gen. 43:11), and admired for the beauty of its blossom, which was depicted in the decorations for the Ark (Ex. 25:33–34).

Almond tree

Apple

Apart from the figurative use of "apples of gold" in Proverbs 25:11, the apple tree and its fruit are only mentioned in the Song of Solomon (e.g. 2:3, 7:8). It has been suggested that apricots, citrons, or quinces were intended, but despite the hot, dry climate, apple trees can be cultivated in Israel.

Cedar

The cedar of Lebanon was a large coniferous tree, whose wood was much prized for its strength and durability. It was used in building **David**'s house (2 Sam. 5:11), and both the first and second temples (1 Kgs. 5:6–10; Ezra 3:7). The "cedar wood" burnt in cleansing rituals (e.g. Lev. 14:4–6) was actually the Phoenician juniper.

Oak

Of the three species of oak found in Palestine, the one referred to in the Bible is most likely the Tabor oak. Oaks were used as burial places (Gen. 35:8; 1 Chron. 10:12) and, in times of idolatry, as sacred groves (e.g. Hos. 4:13).

Palm

The date palm flourished particularly in the **Jordan** valley; **Jericho** was known as "the city of palm trees" (2 Chron. 28:15). The date palm is tall and slender and was used as a symbol of grace and uprightness (e.g. Jer. 10:5). It also signified victory and rejoicing (John 12:13; Rev. 7:9).

Sycamore

The sycamore (sycomore in the King James Version) of the Bible must not be confused with the American or European trees of that name. The Egyptian and Palestinian sycamore is a sturdy, fig-bearing evergreen. It was cultivated in Egypt for both timber and fruit, but in Israel mainly for its fruit (e.g. 1 Chron. 27:28; Amos 7:14). **Zaccheus** climbed a sycamore tree in order to get a better view of Jesus (Luke 19:4).

Willow

Willows are commonly found growing next to streams in the Middle East, and biblical references to them usually associate them with water (e.g. Is. 44:4). The "willow of the brook" (e.g. Lev. 23:40) was probably a poplar, as were the willows by the rivers of Babylon (Ps. 137:2).

Palms

LETTER TO THE EPHESIANS

This letter, probably intended for wider circulation than just to the Christians at **Ephesus**, is traditionally ascribed to **Paul**, although some modern scholars believe it to be from another author, drawing on Paul's letter to the Colossians. Its date is AD 61 or 62.

In the first half of his letter, Paul speaks of God's purposes in sending Jesus. He points out that believers are now saved from death and are brought into new life in Christ, and stresses that they are reconciled not only to God but to each other – there can be no racial barriers between Christians. In the last half of the book, Paul talks about the practical applications of the new life in Christ, calling the Ephesians to unity, purity, and love. He talks mystically about marriage, likening it to Christ's relationship with the Church, but goes on to more practical advice about relationships between parents and children, and servants and masters. The book ends with an exhortation to put on the spiritual armor needed to fight against the forces of evil.

LETTER TO THE PHILIPPIANS

The letter was written from prison by **Paul** to the Christians at **Philippi**. The date is uncertain as it is not clear which imprisonment it arises from, but it was probably either AD 58–60 or 61–63.

Paul writes primarily to thank the Philippians for a gift they have sent him, and to recommend his fellow-workers **Timothy** and Epaphroditus to them. He speaks in a very personal manner of his affection and hopes for this church, and expresses his own joy and confidence in the Gospel of Christ. Paul wishes to encourage the Philippians to continue in faith, unity, and humility, but there is also a warning against false teachers.

Finally, brethren, whatsoever things are true, whatsoever things are honest, whatsoever things are just, whatsoever things are pure, whatsoever things are lovely, whatsoever things are of good report; if there be any virtue, and if there be any praise, think on these things.(Phil. 4:8)

The English Bible, a book which, if everything else in our language should perish, would alone suffice to show the whole extent of its beauty and power.
THOMAS BABINGTON MACAULAY 1800–1859

LETTER TO THE COLOSSIANS

This letter was almost certainly written by **Paul** from prison in Rome around AD 60. It is addressed to the Church at Colossae.

One of the reasons for the letter was to refute false teachings. The Colossians had apparently been influenced by those who had a theory that there was a whole hierarchy of spiritual powers and who advocated the worship of angels. The other strand of false teaching advocated excessive asceticism and strict observance of religious rituals. Paul reminds them of the unique position of Jesus as God's Son and points out that holiness consists of allowing Christ to rule over one's thoughts, passions, and actions. The letter includes some advice for husbands and wives, parents and children, and masters and servants.

LETTERS TO THE THESSALONIANS

These two letters to the Christians at Thessalonica are the earliest of **Paul**'s epistles and date from AD 50 and 51.

Paul writes his first letter to express his pleasure at the good report of these Christians that he has heard from **Timothy**, and to encourage them in the face of possible persecution. After an exhortation to live a chaste and holy life, he moves on to the subject of the Second Coming, assuring them that Christians who have died before this event will have the same status as those who are alive. He continues the theme in the second letter, for apparently some of the Thessalonians had come to believe that the Second Coming was so imminent that there was no need to bother to work. Paul points out that certain signs must precede Christ's coming again and until then they must work diligently.

LETTERS TO TIMOTHY

The two letters to **Timothy** and the letter to Titus are known as the "pastoral epistles," being largely concerned with the care and running of the Church. Though traditionally ascribed to **Paul**, some scholars now believe the letters to have been written some years after Paul's death.

They are addressed to **Timothy**, Paul's close friend and protégé, and contain much of a personal nature. Paul writes to encourage his rather timid friend to be strong and courageous in the faith, and firm in refuting any false teachings. The first letter contains instructions about the conduct of worship and discipline within the Church, and ends with a recommendation to godliness as against materialism. The second letter contains more personal advice and encouragement for Timothy, and includes some predictions about the last days.

For the love of money is the root of all evil. (1 Tim. 6:10)

LETTER TO TITUS

The third "pastoral epistle" (*see* **Letters to Timothy**).

Titus was a pagan convert who had worked closely with Paul and had helped him to establish a church in Crete. In this letter, Paul gives Titus practical advice as to what sort of people he should appoint to positions of leadership in the church. He also warns Titus of the dangers of the false teachers to be found in Crete and urges him to oppose their teachings. Paul gives recommendations as to how various kinds of Christian should conduct their lives and instructs Titus to reject unrepentant heretics.

Unto the pure all things are pure; but unto them that are defiled and unbelieving is nothing pure. (Titus 1:15)

LETTER TO PHILEMON

This is a short personal letter written by **Paul** to a friend, Philemon, living at Colossae. It was written from prison about AD 62.

Philemon's slave, Onesimus, had run away from his master and gone to Rome. Here he had met Paul in prison, become a Christian, and developed a friendship with the apostle. Paul eventually sent Onesimus back to Philemon with this letter. Although runaway slaves were liable to severe punishment, Paul does not simply ask for mercy for Onesimus in the letter; he asks Philemon to treat him like a dear brother, for they are now fellow-Christians.

LETTER TO THE HEBREWS

This letter to Jewish Christians has traditionally been ascribed to **Paul**, but it is now almost universally agreed to have been written after his death at any time between AD 67 and 90.

The primary purpose of the letter appears to be that of persuading Jewish Christians of the unique claims of Jesus and discouraging them from returning to Judaism. The argument begins by presenting Jesus as superior to the angels, to the Old Testament prophets, and to **Moses** and **Joshua**. The next section speaks of Jesus as the great high priest appointed by God. Jesus has offered himself as the supreme and perfect sacrifice and no other sacrifice is now necessary. The author then urges the Hebrews to hold fast to their new faith, and invokes various Old Testament heroes to inspire them to greater faith. The final chapter is concerned with practical advice and exhortation.

Now faith is the substance of things hoped for, the evidence of things not seen. (Heb. 11:1)

S. TITUS
BISHOP of CRETE.

MICHAEL BURGHERS DELINE. ET SCULP.

S. Titus

LETTER FROM JAMES

This letter, addressed to the dispersed Jewish Christians, has been assumed to have been written by **James**, Jesus' brother, around AD 50, although some scholars maintain that it was written by another James, forty or fifty years later.

Its emphasis is on the ethical behavior appropriate to Christians, particularly in regard to their attitude to money. James points out the hypocrisy of those who appear to be religious but neglect the poor, or those who pay respect to the rich and despise poor people. His doctrine is that "faith without works is dead": Christians prove that they have faith by showing compassion to the needy. After a digression about wisdom and the need to control our speech and thoughts, James returns to a fierce attack on rich people who oppress and neglect the poor, but ends on a gentler note with exhortations to pray for one another.

Pure religion and undefiled before God and the Father is this, to visit the fatherless and widows in their affliction, and to keep himself unspotted from the world. (Jas. 1:27)

LETTERS FROM PETER

The first letter from **Peter**, to Jewish Christians dispersed throughout five provinces, is almost certainly the work of the apostle Peter, and probably dates from AD 64. The second letter is very unlikely to have been written by the apostle, and probably dates from the second century AD.

In the first letter, there is a stress on the theme of suffering and trials of faith, for Peter was writing against a background of persecution of Christians. He exhorts them to faith and godliness and reminds them of the honor and privilege of being among the people of God. He urges them to follow Christ's example in withstanding suffering and false accusations. After some advice on the duties of husbands and wives, Peter returns to the theme of imminent suffering. The second letter contains a denunciation of false prophets and teachers, and a reminder of the certainty of the Second Coming.

… one day is with the Lord as a thousand years, and a thousand years as one day. (2 Pet. 3:8)

LETTERS FROM JOHN

These three letters are thought to be addressed to churches around **Ephesus**. They are all thought to be from the same hand, and very likely by the writer of

Basilica of St John at Ephesus (AD 527–565)

the Gospel of John. This writer was probably not the apostle, but an associate of his, who was an elder of the Ephesian Church. The date of writing is estimated as around AD 90.

There is no personal content in 1 John, which reads more like a sermon than a letter. Its main theme is an attack on heresy, in particular the heresy being put about by a group of false teachers attempting to influence the Church at that time. John argues forcefully that Jesus was and is the Messiah, God's Son, who came in the flesh to bring salvation. Reiterating a theme of John's Gospel, the writer says that God is light, and exhorts his readers to walk in the light and to hate the darkness of sin. He speaks of the love of God and urges Christians to love one another and keep God's commandments. The second letter is addressed to "the elect lady and her children," but this is thought to refer not to individuals but to a church. John warns again of false teachers, and again urges Christians to love. The third letter is addressed to Gaius, a church elder, commending him for his adherence to truth and his hospitable habits. These are contrasted with the arrogance of one Diotrophes, who was apparently causing trouble in the church.

Beloved, let us love one another: for love is of God; and every one that loveth is born of God and knoweth God … for God is love. (1 John 4:7–8)

LETTER FROM JUDE

This short letter is usually thought to have been written by Jude or Judas, the brother of Jesus, between AD 70 and 80, although some ascribe it to an unknown author of the second century AD.

The primary message is a denunciation of false

*Engraving by Albrecht Dürer
(1471–1528) illustrating the
book of Revelation*

teachers. Jude predicts the downfall of these men by using examples from the Old Testament to show that God's judgment on the wicked is sure and inevitable. He urges his readers to protect themselves against such false teaching by building themselves up in faith by prayer, and to rescue those who are led astray.

REVELATION OF JOHN

This book was originally ascribed to the apostle **John**. Later scholars thought it more likely to have come from the elder John who also probably wrote the Gospel and the letters of John, but many now think the author was a different person writing near the end of the first century AD.

This book is unlike any other in the Bible. It is a mystical, apocalyptic work, using imagery and symbolism that is difficult for modern readers to interpret. The author, exiled on the island of Patmos, has a vision of the resurrected Jesus, who gives him messages for seven churches: at **Ephesus**, Smyrna, Pergamum, Thyatira, Sardis, Philadelphia, and Laodicea. Individual messages of encouragement or reproof are sent to each church. The following chapters are an account of John's vision, in which he sees a lamb opening a book with seven seals; four horsemen symbolizing conquest, slaughter, famine, and death; seven trumpets, each preceding a vision; war in heaven between Satan and the angels; and the beast whose number is 666. He then describes a series of plagues and a scarlet woman who, with Babylon, is to be destroyed. The final chapters speak of the millennium, when Satan is bound for a thousand years and Christ prevails, and John's vision of the new Jerusalem.

And God shall wipe away all tears from their eyes; and there shall be no more death, neither sorrow, nor crying, neither shall there be any more pain: for the former things are passed away. (Rev. 21:4)

***Above** Illustrations of the book of Revelation from the first edition Luther Bible of 1534. The top picture shows the Last Judgment (Rev. 14), the middle picture illustrates the reaper (Rev. 14:14), and the bottom picture shows the key of the bottomless pit (Rev. 20:18)*

BIBLE CHARACTERS

All of the most important – and interesting –

characters in the Old and New Testaments have

been selected for this "Who's Who" of the

Bible. Characters are listed in the order in

which they appear and major Bible references

are given.

***Left** Adoring Saints from the left*
panel of the San Pier Maggiore
Altarpiece, by Jacopo di Cione
(active 1365–98)

BIBLE CHARACTERS

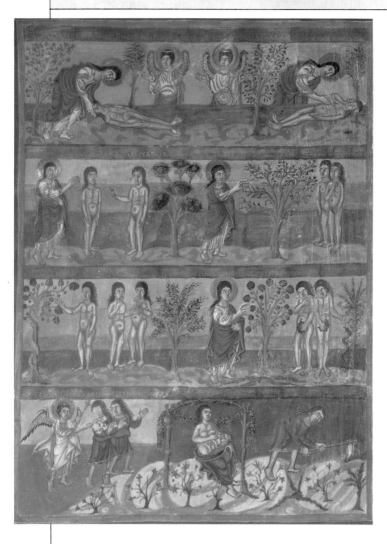

Illustration from the ninth-century French Grandval Bible, showing the creation, temptation, and fall of Adam and Eve

No man, who knows nothing else, knows even his Bible.
MATTHEW ARNOLD 1822–1888

The Bible is literature, not dogma.
GEORGE SANTAYANA 1863–1952

ADAM

Meaning of name: Earth, man
Bible reference: Gen. 2–3, 4:1, 25, 5:1–4

The first man, Adam was created out of dust by God and was given the task of naming and ruling over all the animals. He and his wife **Eve** were placed in the beautiful and fruitful garden of Eden and told that they could eat fruit from every tree, except the tree of the knowledge of good and evil. First Eve, and then Adam, succumbed to temptation and ate this fruit, as a result of which·they became aware of their nakedness and made themselves clothes from fig leaves. When God accused him of disobedience Adam blamed Eve, but God cast them both out of·the garden.

EVE

Meaning of name: Life
Bible reference: Gen. 2: 18–4:2

The first woman. According to one account she was made in God's image at the same time as man; the other account has her created from **Adam**'s rib. Eve was deceived by the serpent into disobeying God's commandment: she ate the forbidden fruit and then offered it to Adam. Before he cast them out of the garden (*see* **Adam**) God told Eve that she would now suffer in childbirth and be subject to her husband.

CAIN

Meaning of name: Acquisition
Bible reference: Gen. 4

The eldest son of **Adam** and **Eve**, and the first murderer. Cain was jealous when his brother **Abel**'s offering of a lamb was preferred by God to his own offering of crops, and he killed his brother. When God asked him where Abel was, Cain replied, "Am I my brother's keeper?" God told Cain that from then on he would become a permanent fugitive, but set a mark upon him so that he should not be killed.

ABEL

Meaning of name: Meadow, breath, *or* vanity
Bible reference: Gen. 4:2–9

The second son of **Adam** and **Eve**. He became a shepherd and God was pleased with the offering of his first-born lamb as a sacrifice. Abel was subsequently murdered by his angry and jealous brother Cain, whose own offering to God had been rejected. God was pleased with this offering but rejected the offering that Abel's brother **Cain** brought.

NOAH

Meaning of name: Rest
Bible reference: Gen. 5:28–9:29

An early patriarch. Noah was a good and just man at a time of great wickedness. God regretted having created humankind and planned to destroy all living things by a flood, but he decided to save Noah and his family. He gave Noah instructions for building an ark to accommodate himself, his wife, his sons and their wives, and two of each animal. Noah built the ark, and when the rains came he, his family, and the animals were saved, but everyone else was destroyed. After seven months the ark came to rest on the top of Mount Ararat. Noah sent out a dove and it returned with an olive leaf, so they knew that the flood had abated. God made a covenant with Noah that he would never again destroy the world by flood, and the sign of the covenant was a rainbow.

The story of Noah is one of the best-loved in the Bible. This early twentieth-century representation of Noah's ark is by Gladys Hynes

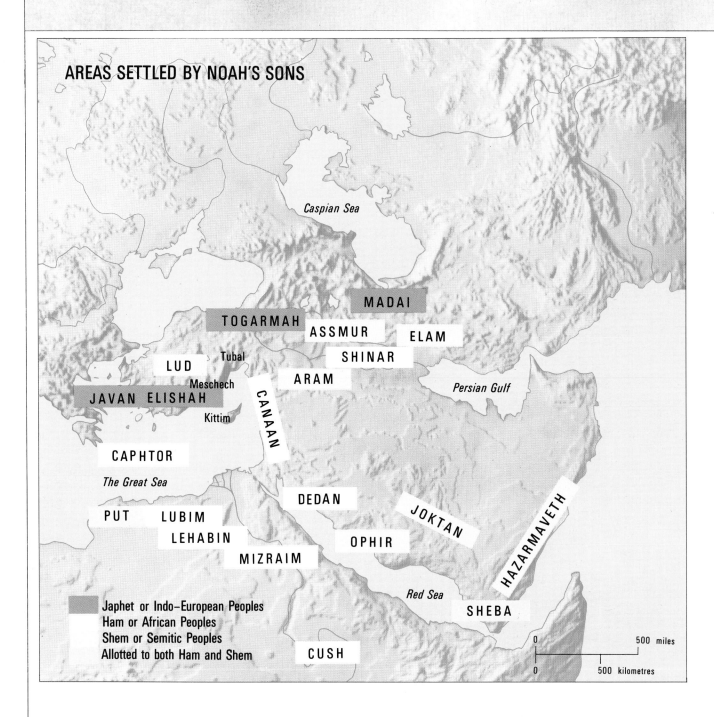

AREAS SETTLED BY NOAH'S SONS

Caspian Sea

MADAI

TOGARMAH

ASSMUR

ELAM

SHINAR

Tubal

LUD

ARAM

Meschech

JAVAN ELISHAH

Persian Gulf

CANAAN

Kittim

CAPHTOR

The Great Sea

DEDAN

JOKTAN

PUT   LUBIM

HAZARMAVETH

LEHABIN

OPHIR

MIZRAIM

Red Sea

SHEBA

Japhet or Indo–European Peoples
Ham or African Peoples
Shem or Semitic Peoples
Allotted to both Ham and Shem

CUSH

0   500 miles

0   500 kilometres

The area settled by Noah's sons, as described in the "table of nations" (Gen. 10)

ABRAHAM

Meaning of name: Father of a multitude
Bible reference: Gen. 11:27–25:10

Abraham was a descendant of **Noah**. He was born in **Ur** in **Babylonia** but his family moved to **Haran**. Abraham prospered there but when he was seventy-five years old God told him to leave Haran and travel to **Canaan**. God promised Abraham that he would become the father of a great nation and, as a sign of this

Left *Early sixteenth century*
Italian dish illustrating the story
of Abraham's sacrifice of his son
Isaac

Below Lot and his Daughters
by Albrecht Dürer (1471–
1528); the picture shows the
family leaving Sodom after its
destruction

covenant, Abraham and all his male descendants were to be circumcised.

Abraham's wife **Sarah** was barren but her servant **Hagar** had borne him a son, **Ishmael**. At last, when Abraham and Sarah were both very old, God promised them a son, and **Isaac** was born. When Isaac was a young man God tested Abraham's faith and obedience by commanding him to take Isaac up a mountain and offer him as a sacrifice. Abraham obeyed but, as he was about to kill his son, he was stopped by an angel, and God provided a ram to sacrifice in Isaac's place.

Abraham was the ancestor of all the Hebrew people and Isaiah 41 refers to him as God's friend.

LOT

Meaning of name: Covering *or* concealed
Bible reference: Gen. 11:27,31, 12:5, 13, 14:12–16, 19

Nephew of **Abraham**. He accompanied Abraham to **Canaan** but they separated and Lot elected to live in the fruitful **Jordan** valley. He settled among the notorious people of **Sodom**, but was rescued by angels when the city was destroyed by God. Lot protected the angels whom he was entertaining from the lust of the men of Sodom, but his virtue is diminished by the fact that he offered his daughters instead. When they escaped the destruction of the city, Lot's wife looked back, and was turned into a pillar of salt. Making their father drunk, Lot's daughters conceived sons by him, who became the ancestors of the Moabites and the Ammonites.

SARAH

Meaning of name: Princess
Bible reference: Gen. 11:29–30, 12:11–20, 16:1–6, 17:15–19, 18:1–15, 20, 21:1–10, 23:1–2, 19

Wife of **Abraham**. Sarah was also Abraham's half-sister and on two occasions during their travels Abraham pretended she was his sister, for he was afraid that her great beauty might endanger his safety. Sarah was childless for many years, but when she was an old woman Abraham entertained three angels who declared that she would have a son. Sarah laughed when she heard this, but she gave birth to **Isaac**. (*See also* **Hagar, Ishmael.**)

Abraham Turning Away Hagar *by Emile Jean Horace Vernet (1789–1863). Abraham,* *to please Sarah, is banishing Hagar and their son Ishmael (Gen. 21:8–14)*

HAGAR

Meaning of name: Flight
Bible reference: Gen. 16, 21:9–21

Egyptian handmaid of **Sarah**. When Sarah was unable to conceive, she gave Hagar to **Abraham** as a concubine. Hagar became pregnant, which made her despise her mistress. Sarah treated her harshly and Hagar fled, but she met an angel who told her to return. Hagar had a son, **Ishmael**, but after her own son was born Sarah cast Hagar and Ishmael out. In the wilderness they ran out of water, and Hagar left her son, for she did not want to witness his death. Then God spoke to her and she saw a well of water; she and Ishmael drank and were saved.

ISHMAEL

Meaning of name: God hears
Bible reference: Gen. 16:3–4, 15, 17:18, 20, 23–27, 21:9–21, 25:12–18, 28:9

Son of **Abraham** and **Hagar**. When Hagar fled from **Sarah** (*see* **Hagar**), the angel who appeared to her told her that the son she would bear would be called Ishmael, and would be a wild man whom everyone would oppose. When **Isaac** was weaned, his father gave a feast and Sarah saw Ishmael mocking. He and his mother were cast out to wander in the wilderness. Ishmael grew up, became an archer, and married an Egyptian woman.

ISAAC

Meaning of name: Laughter
Bible reference: Gen. 18:1–15, 21:1–8, 22:1–19, 24, 25:11, 19–26, 26:1–28:8, 35:27–29

Son of **Abraham** and **Sarah**. The much-loved child of his parents' old age, Isaac came close to death when his father was commanded to sacrifice him (*see* **Abraham**). He was married to **Rebekah**, his cousin's daughter, and was the only one of the patriarchs to be monogamous. God blessed Isaac with great prosperity, but in his old age he appeared to dwell on more material things, for it was his love of venison that drew him to **Esau** and led to his giving the wrong son his blessing (*see* **Esau**).

REBEKAH

Meaning of name: Noose
Bible reference: Gen. 24:15–67, 25:20–24, 28, 26:35, 27:5–17, 42–46

Wife of **Isaac**. **Abraham** sent his most trusted servant to look for a wife for **Isaac** and when he stopped at a well, Rebekah offered him water and hospitality at her father's house. The servant realized that she was related to his master and he arranged a marriage between her and Isaac. Rebekah was barren for twenty years until she gave birth to the twins **Esau** and **Jacob**. Rebekah loved Jacob best and it was she who planned the tricking of Isaac over Esau's blessing (*see* **Esau**).

ESAU

Meaning of name: Hairy
Bible reference: Gen. 25:21–34, 26:34–27:46, 28:6–9, 32–33, 35:29–36:19

Elder son of **Isaac** and **Rebekah**. Esau became a hunter and his father's favorite. Being the first-born of twins, Esau was entitled to the birthright, but he sold it to his brother, **Jacob**, in return for some lentil stew.

Esau was then tricked out of his father's blessing by Jacob and Rebekah. Isaac had asked Esau to bring venison and make him a stew from it, so he could eat and then bless his son before he died. But Rebekah made a stew and covered Jacob in goat skin so that he would feel hairy like his brother. Jacob then pretended to be Esau and obtained the blessing. Esau hated Jacob for this, and wanted to kill him, but eventually the brothers were reconciled.

JACOB

Meaning of name: Follower, supplanter
Bible reference: Gen. 25:21–34, 27–35, 37:1, 3, 10, 31–35, 42:1–4, 29–38, 43:1–14, 46–49

Second son of **Isaac** and **Rebekah**. He cheated his twin brother out of his birthright and his father's blessing (*see* **Esau**). After the latter episode, Jacob fled from Esau's wrath to take refuge with his uncle Laban. On his way he dreamed that he saw a ladder reaching up to heaven and that God promised to be with him. Jacob fell in love with Laban's younger daughter, **Rachel**, but Laban tricked him into marrying her sister as well (*see* **Leah**). Jacob became very rich and had twelve sons by his two wives and two concubines. After twenty years, he and his family left Laban to return to **Canaan**; on the way Jacob wrestled with a strange man, apparently an angel, who renamed him Israel.

Above Jacob Wrestling with the Angel *by Rembrandt (1606–69). The picture illustrates the incident described in Genesis 32: 24–29*

Below When the Israelies entered Canaan the land was apportioned between twelve separate tribes. These tribes were the descendants of the twelve sons of Jacob. The chart illustrates how the tribes are descended from Terah on both sides, through family intermarriage

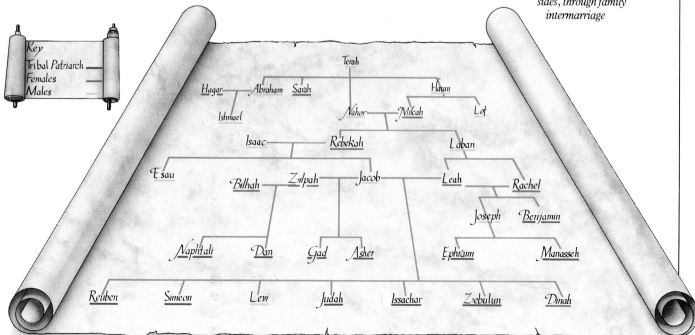

RACHEL

Meaning of name: Ewe
Bible reference: Gen. 29, 30:1–24, 31:4–19, 33–35, 33:1, 7, 35:16–20; Jer. 31:15

Wife of **Jacob**. When Jacob traveled to **Haran** to stay with his uncle Laban, the first person he met was Laban's younger daughter Rachel, who was taking her father's sheep to water. Rachel was beautiful and Jacob fell in love with her, but was tricked into marrying her sister first (*see* **Leah**). Rachel was childless for many years, although Jacob fathered sons on her handmaid, Bilhah, but at last she gave birth to **Joseph**. Rachel did not share her husband's devotion to God for, when they left Laban, she stole her father's household gods and when he pursued them she hid the images so he could not find them. Rachel died giving birth to Benjamin, the youngest of Jacob's sons.

LEAH

Meaning of name: Cow
Bible reference: Gen. 29:16–35, 30:9–21, 49:31

Wife of **Jacob**. Leah was the elder daughter of Laban. Jacob fell in love with her sister **Rachel** and agreed to serve Laban for seven years to earn her. After this time Jacob claimed Rachel as his wife, but on the wedding night Laban substituted Leah for her sister – a trick which Jacob did not realize until the morning. Jacob was allowed to marry Rachel too but had to serve Laban another seven years for her. There was considerable jealousy between the sisters, Leah envying Rachel because Jacob loved her best, and Rachel envying Leah her fertility.

JOSEPH

Meaning of name: God increases
Bible reference: Gen. 30:22–24, 37, 39–50

Son of **Jacob** and **Rachel**. Joseph incurred the hatred of his older brothers because of his father's favoritism and because of his own dreams, in which he appeared to be prophesying that he would rule over them. They considered killing him but finally sold him to some

Illustrations from the Golden Haggadah, a medieval Jewish manuscript, showing incidents from the life of Joseph

merchants, although they told **Jacob** that he had been killed by wild animals.

Joseph was taken into **Egypt** and sold to Potiphar, one of Pharaoh's officers. He found favor with Potiphar and was promoted to overseer, but when he rejected the advances of Potiphar's wife she pretended he had assaulted her, and he was imprisoned. While in prison he successfully interpreted his fellow-prisoners' dreams, and when Pharaoh had a dream Joseph was summoned to interpret it. The interpretation was that there would be plentiful years followed by famine, and Joseph advised Pharaoh to store grain during the good years. Pharaoh agreed and appointed Joseph as governor. He became rich and powerful, and when his brothers arrived in Egypt to buy corn they failed to recognize him. Joseph eventually revealed himself and told his brothers he forgave them because God had blessed him so greatly.

MOSES

Meaning of name: Child *or* drawn forth
Bible reference: Ex. 2–40; Lev. 1:1; Num. 1–36; Deut. 1–34

Leader and lawgiver. Adopted by Pharaoh's daughter (*see* **Miriam**), Moses had a privileged upbringing, but he identified with his own people and resented their

oppression by the Egyptians. He was forced to flee to **Midian** after killing an Egyptian who was beating a Hebrew slave. While he was in Midian, God spoke to Moses from a miraculously burning bush, and told him to return to **Egypt** and liberate his people.

Moses asked Pharaoh to let the people leave Egypt and, when Pharaoh refused, God visited the Egyptians with plagues of frogs, flies, locusts, boils, and hailstorms. The rivers turned to blood, there was darkness over the land, and the animals all died; but not until God killed all the first-born sons of the Egyptians did Pharaoh agree to let the Hebrew people go. After they left, the Egyptians pursued them to the Red Sea. God told Moses to hold his hand over the sea. The waters divided and the Hebrews crossed the sea, but when the Egyptians followed they were drowned.

At Mount **Sinai** God gave Moses the laws that the people were to obey, including the Ten Commandments. Moses led the people through the desert for forty years as spiritual and military leader, until they reached the land God had promised them, but Moses himself did not enter the land.

AARON

Meaning of name: Mountain
Bible reference: Ex. 4:14–16, 5:1, 17:12, 28, 29, 32; Num. 12, 17–20

The elder brother of **Moses**. He was chosen by God to be Moses' spokesman because of his eloquence, and was the first high priest of Israel. It was Aaron who was responsible for making the golden calf which the Israelites worshiped while Moses was on Mount **Sinai**.

Moses Rescued from the Nile
by Paolo Veronese (c. 1528–88): a very sixteenth-century representation of the story in Exodus 2:5 where Pharoah's daughter instructs her maids to take the baby from the river

Thirteenth-century stained glass from Chartres Cathedral, depicting the high priest Aaron

MIRIAM

Meaning of name: Beloved *or* bitter
Bible reference: Ex. 2:4–8, 15:20–21; Num. 12, 20:1; Deut. 24:9; Mic. 6:4

Sister of **Moses** and **Aaron**. The family lived in **Egypt**, and Moses was born at a time when the Pharaoh had ordered all male Hebrew babies to be killed. Their mother hid Moses in a basket and left it by the river. When Pharaoh's daughter found the baby, Miriam offered to find him a nurse, and fetched her mother to nurse Moses. Miriam became a prophetess and led the women in celebrating their crossing of the Red Sea. Miriam and Aaron later rebelled against Moses, and God punished Miriam with leprosy, but healed her after seven days.

Right Sixteenth-century German stained glass showing the miracle of the fleece, by which God confirmed Gideon's call (*Judg. 6*)

Far right Samson and Delilah *by Andrea Mantegna (1431–1506). Delilah is fastening Samson's hair with a pin (Judg. 16:14)*

JOSHUA

Meaning of name: God is salvation
Bible reference: Ex. 17:9–16, 24:13, 33:11; Num. 13:1–16, 14:6–9, 27:18–23; Deut. 31:23; Josh. 1–24

Soldier and leader. Joshua was chosen as a helper by **Moses**. He was one of the spies sent to report on the land of **Canaan** and only he and Caleb urged Moses to go in and possess it. He was appointed as successor to Moses and led the people after Moses' death, commanding several successful campaigns against the Canaanites. Joshua's military feats were matched by his trust in God which resulted in some spectacular events, such as the fall of the walls of **Jericho**, and the sun and moon standing still at Joshua's command.

RAHAB

Meaning of name: Broad
Bible reference: Josh. 2, 6:17, 22–25

A prostitute of **Jericho**. **Joshua** sent out two spies to Jericho and they lodged with Rahab. The king heard that they were there and sent to Rahab's house for them. Rahab believed that God had given the Israelites the land of **Canaan**, and she wanted them to succeed in their attempt to seize it. She lied to those who came in search of the spies, and helped the men to escape, letting them out through a back window. She asked only that she and her family should be saved when the city was destroyed, and Joshua saw that this was done.

DEBORAH

Meaning of name: Bee
Bible reference: Judg. 4–5

Judge and prophetess. Deborah was the fifth of the leaders of Israel appointed by God after the invasion of **Canaan** and before the monarchy was established. Most of these "judges" were military leaders but Deborah acted as a civil judge too. She was a fervent patriot who commanded the warrior Barak to go to Mount Tabor to fight against Sisera's army. Barak refused to go unless Deborah went with him. Sisera's whole army was killed and Deborah's song celebrates this event.

GIDEON

Meaning of name: Hewer
Bible reference: Judg. 6-8

Fifth judge of Israel. Gideon was of obscure birth; although his father was a worshiper of Baal, he himself believed in God. Informed by an angel that God had chosen him to defeat the Midianites, who were ruling Israel at that time, Gideon gathered an army together. To make quite sure that God was really going to use him, Gideon asked God for a sign. He placed a fleece on the ground and told God that if, in the morning, there was dew on the fleece but not on the ground, he would believe he was chosen. This happened, but Gideon asked God to reverse the miracle. Next morning there was dew on the ground but not on the fleece. God then told Gideon that his army was too large. Following God's instructions, Gideon reduced it to just three hundred, and with this tiny army he defeated the Midianites.

SAMSON

Meaning of name: Of the sun
Bible reference: Judg. 13-16

Judge of Israel. At the time of the Philistine oppression, an angel appeared to a barren Hebrew woman and told her that she would bear a son who must never cut his hair because he would be dedicated to God, and would deliver Israel from the Philistines. The son was Samson, who became an extraordinarily strong man and judge of Israel. His marriage to a Philistine woman grieved his parents and resulted in the slaughter of a thousand Philistines. Later he fell in love with **Delilah**, who betrayed him (*see* **Delilah**) so that his hair was cut off and he was captured by the Philistines. The

Philistine rulers met to celebrate Samson's downfall and decided to have him brought out of prison to entertain them. Samson's hair had grown again while he was in prison and he had regained his strength. After praying for revenge, he pushed against the pillars that held the building up. The building collapsed, killing Samson and three thousand Philistines.

DELILAH

Meaning of name: Delicate
Bible reference: Judg. 16:4–22

A Philistine woman, mistress of **Samson**. Samson, judge of Israel, fell in love with Delilah. She was bribed by his enemies, the Philistine kings, to find out the secret of Samson's strength, so they could overpower him. Three times Delilah asked Samson to tell her the secret of his strength and each time he gave her a false answer. Delilah complained that Samson did not really love her and nagged him so much that at last he revealed that his strength was in his hair, which had never been cut. Delilah lulled Samson to sleep. While he slept, his enemies cut off his hair, and he was captured and blinded.

Nineteenth-century stained glass window by R. T. Bayne, showing Ruth gleaning in Boaz's fields

RUTH

Meaning of name: Friend
Bible reference: Ruth 1–4

A Moabite woman, great-grandmother of **David**. When Naomi decided to leave Moab to return to **Bethlehem** (*see* **Naomi**), she expected her daughters-in-law to remain and remarry. But Ruth insisted on going with Naomi, saying, "thy people shall be my people, and thy God my God." Ruth went to glean corn in the field belonging to **Boaz** (*see* **Boaz**). Obeying Naomi's instructions, Ruth lay at Boaz's feet as he slept and, when he woke, claimed his protection as a kinsman. After a nearer kinsman had rejected the opportunity, Boaz redeemed Naomi's property and married Ruth.

NAOMI

Meaning of name: Pleasant, my delight
Bible reference: Ruth 1–4

Mother-in-law of **Ruth**. She came from **Bethlehem**, but her family moved to **Moab** in a time of famine and her sons married Moabite women, Ruth and Orpah. Naomi's husband and sons died and she resolved to return to Bethlehem alone, but Ruth insisted on going with her. Naomi planned the marriage between Ruth and **Boaz**, and when their son Obed was born she took on the responsibility of his care.

BOAZ

Meaning of name: Strength
Bible reference: Ruth 2–4

Husband of **Ruth**. Boaz was a rich landlord related to the father of Ruth's first husband, who had died. Ruth's mother-in-law, **Naomi**, sent Ruth to glean corn in Boaz's field and Boaz offered her protection and hospitality. His sense of family responsibility, and also perhaps an inclination toward Ruth, led him to redeem her property when a nearer kinsman refused to do so. Boaz then married Ruth, and became the great-grandfather of **David**.

HANNAH

Meaning of name: Grace
Bible reference: 1 Sam. 1, 2:1–10, 18–21

Mother of **Samuel**. Hannah was grieved because of her childlessness and she vowed to God that if he gave her a son she would dedicate him to God's service. Soon after, she became pregnant, and when Samuel was weaned, she took him to the priest **Eli** to be brought up in the house of the Lord. Hannah visited Samuel every year, always bringing a coat she had made for him; she subsequently had five more children. Hannah's song of thanksgiving exalts God for his holiness, power, and faithfulness to the weak and lowly.

SAMUEL

Meaning of name: Heard by God
Bible reference: 1 Sam. 1–3, 7–12, 15–16, 25:1

Prophet and judge. Dedicated to God by his mother (*see* **Hannah**), Samuel was brought up in the house of the priest **Eli**. God spoke to him when he was still a boy, prophesying doom for Eli's family (*see* **Eli**). Samuel became judge and leader over Israel, gathering an army that defeated the Philistines. When the people demanded a king, Samuel resisted their wishes at first, but God gave him instructions to anoint **Saul**, which he did. Samuel fell out with Saul because of his disobedience of God's commandments, and he secretly anointed **David**.

ELI

Meaning of name: God is high
Bible reference: 1 Sam. 1:9–4:18

Judge and high priest of Israel. Eli was of the tribe of Levi and his priesthood was a hereditary office. Although Eli himself lived a blameless life, his sons abused their priesthoods and behaved scandalously. Eli was grieved by their behavior, but barely reproached them for it. The child **Samuel** heard a message from God pronouncing the downfall of Eli and his sons, because of their wickedness and his failure to rebuke them effectively. The sons were killed by the Philistines and the ark of the covenant was taken. When he heard this news, Eli fell from his seat, breaking his neck, and died.

The Bible is no mere book, but a living creature, with a power that conquers all that oppose it.
NAPOLEON BONAPARTE 1769–1821

PAGAN DEITIES IN THE BIBLE

The first of the Ten Commandments forbids the worship of any other gods beside Jehovah. The Bible frequently mentions such gods and the cults that surrounded them. Those discussed below are probably the most important of the many referred to.

GODS OF THE ISRAELITES, CANAANITES, AND NEIGHBORING PEOPLES

The Baal cult has its origin in the worship of a Semitic storm god. This copper figure shows a Canaanite Baal deity with an arm raised to hold a spear, which represented lightning

The Semitic god most mentioned in the Old Testament is Baal, although in fact *ba'al* is a Hebrew word meaning "master" or "possessor" and the title became attached to various local gods. The most important baal in **Canaan** was related to Hadad, the Syrian thunder god. At the time the Israelites entered Canaan, worship of this baal was well established, and the word became used for Jehovah (Hos. 2:16–17). This soon led to confusion between the rituals of Baal worship and Jehovah worship, and worship of Baal became rife among the Hebrew people (e.g. Judg. 2:11–13). The various baals were usually fertility or nature gods, closely connected with the elements.

The consort of Baal was the goddess whom the Hebrews called Ashteroth and the Canaanites Asherah. The word "Asherah" is frequently used in the Old Testament to refer to a wooden image of the goddess, although in the King James Version the translation is always given as "grove" (e.g. Deut. 16:21). She was a goddess of erotic love and fertility, and her cults often involved ritual prostitution.

This stained glass picture shows the wrath of Moses as he returned from Sinai to find the Israelites worshiping a golden calf (Ex. 32)

Another object of idolatrous worship was the golden calf, which the Israelites made and **Moses** destroyed (Ex. 32). They may have been influenced by the bull cult surrounding the Egyptian god Horus, or possibly by a similar cult linked to the Canaanite Baal.

The Israelites were exposed to various pagan religions embraced by their neighbors. The god Moloch, Molech, or Milcom was worshiped by the Ammonites (1 Kgs. 11:7). His cult involved child sacrifice and was apparently adopted by some Hebrews, as it is specifically forbidden in Leviticus 18:21. The cult of child sacrifice was also associated with the Moabite god Chemosh (Num. 21:29). The Philistine god was Dagon, supposed to have been a fish god, and worshiped at the time of **Samson** and **Saul** (e.g. Judg. 16:23; 1 Sam. 5:2–7).

MESOPOTAMIAN GODS

Assyrian religion differed little from that of Babylon and the two can be considered together. The principal deity was Bel (baal) or Marduk, a warrior god (Jer. 50:2), who features in the apocryphal story of Bel and the Dragon. His son was Nabu, or Nebo, who was the god of science and learning (Is. 46:1).

The principal goddess of the region was Ishtar, who equated with Ashteroth and was goddess of love and war. She was closely associated with her husband Tammuz (Ezek. 8:14), a fertility god whose supposed death and resurrection explained the cycle of vegetation.

Other deities included Rimmon, a title of the thunder god Hadad, who was worshiped particularly at **Damascus** (2 Kgs. 5:17–18). Nisroch was the god worshiped by King Sennacherib (2 Kgs. 19:37), and Nergal was the god of the underworld, worshiped throughout Assyria and Babylon, but particularly at Cuthah (2 Kgs. 17:30).

GREEK AND ROMAN GODS

There is no indication that the worship of Baal and similar gods survived into New Testament times among the Jews in Israel. However, when **Paul** and others began their missionary work, it was the gods of the Greek and Roman pantheon who had to be confronted. The many warnings against idolatry in the letters of Paul and John would presumably have referred to these gods.

When Paul and **Barnabas** visited **Lystra** and Paul healed a crippled man, the people hailed them as gods, calling Paul Mercury and Barnabas Jupiter (Acts 14:8–12). Jupiter (or Zeus in Greece) was the supreme god of Rome and Greece, a god of thunder and king of the gods. Mercury, or Hermes, was his messenger, and the god of science and commerce.

This statue of Diana or Artemis comes from Ephesus, which was the center of the cult surrounding her. Her temple there was one of the seven wonders of the world. The multiple breasts symbolize fertility

The daughter of Zeus was Diana, or Artemis. She was goddess of the moon and of hunting. Although her cult became associated with virginity, she is thought to have been originally a fertility goddess. At Ephesus, where Paul fell foul of her followers (Acts 19:23–29), worship of Artemis had become confused with worship of a local mother goddess, and the goddess was portrayed with many breasts, symbolizing fertility.

Although David had a long and eventful reign as king of Israel and Judah, he is still most popularly remembered as the young slayer of the giant Goliath. This picture by Philippe le Bel de Breviare shows David with Saul and Goliath

SAUL

Meaning of name: Asked for
Bible reference: 1 Sam. 9–11, 13–24, 26–28, 31; 2 Sam. 1

First king of Israel. Anointed as king by **Samuel**, Saul became a great military leader. Though originally filled with the Spirit of God, Saul became increasingly disobedient to God's commandments and God rejected him as king. Once God's Spirit had left him, Saul became prey to fits of melancholy and the young **David** was summoned to play the harp to him, which soothed him. After David's victory over **Goliath**, and his increasing popularity with the people, Saul was consumed with jealousy and hatred for him. He sought for many years to kill David though thwarted by his own son and daughter (*see* **Jonathan**, **Michal**). When his army was defeated by the Philistines, and his sons were killed, Saul killed himself on the battlefield.

JONATHAN

Meaning of name: The Lord has given
Bible reference: 1 Sam. 13:2–3, 14, 18:1–5, 19:1–7, 20, 31:2; 2 Sam. 1

Son of **Saul**. Jonathan was a fearless soldier and his father's heir. He became a very close friend of **David**, never resenting the ascendency that David gained, and risking his own relationship with his father through his love and loyalty to his friend. He died with his father and brothers, fighting the Philistines.

MICHAL

Meaning of name: Who is like Jehovah?
Bible reference: 1 Sam. 14:49, 18:20–28, 19:11–17, 25:44; 2 Sam. 3:13–14, 6:16–23

A wife of **David**. Michal was **Saul**'s younger daughter. She fell in love with David and her father planned to use this to effect David's downfall. He offered her to David as a bride, but demanded a dowry of a hundred Philistine foreskins. The plan misfired, for David killed twice the required number of Philistines and married Michal. When Saul again attempted to kill David, Michal helped him to escape, deceiving her father. While David was in exile, Saul married Michal to another man, but after Saul's death David demanded her return. Michal despised David for his abandoned dancing when the ark of the Lord was brought into the city, and because of this she remained childless forever.

DAVID

Meaning of name: Beloved
Bible reference: 1 Sam. 16–31; 2 Sam. 1–24; 1 Kgs.
1:1–2:11; 1 Chron. 11–29

Second king of Israel. Descended from **Ruth**, and the youngest of eight brothers, David was brought up as a shepherd. When God rejected **Saul** as king, **Samuel** secretly anointed David. David first came to King Saul's attention as a musician (*see* **Saul**), and then found fame when he killed the Philistine **Goliath** (*see* **Goliath**). Saul's son became David's closest friend and his daughter became his wife (*see* **Jonathan, Michal**), but Saul subsequently turned against David, who spent many years in exile fleeing from the king.

When Saul and Jonathan were killed in battle, David became king and reigned for some forty years. He was noted for his skill as a warrior as well as for his gifts as a prophet and poet. He was devoted to God and recovered the ark of the covenant, bringing it to **Jerusalem**. The psalms that David wrote reveal his great love for and closeness to God, but his saintliness was marred, and the episode of **Uriah** (*see* **Bathsheba, Uriah**) was a shameful one. (*See also* **Abigail, Absalom, Joab.**)

GOLIATH

Meaning of name: Exile
Bible reference: 1 Sam. 17

Giant of Gath. Goliath was a huge man (around ten feet tall) who was fighting for the Philistine army. Heavily armed, he demanded a champion from the Israelites to fight him in single combat. He issued the challenge every day for forty days, until the young **David** volunteered to fight him. Goliath mocked when he saw the unarmed boy coming toward him, but David, using a sling, hit Goliath in the forehead with a stone, breaking his skull and killing him.

Above This gate is traditionally held to be the entrance to David's citadel in Jerusalem

Left A reconstruction of what the Ark of the Covenant might have looked like. King David brought the ark to Jerusalem and established his new capital city there

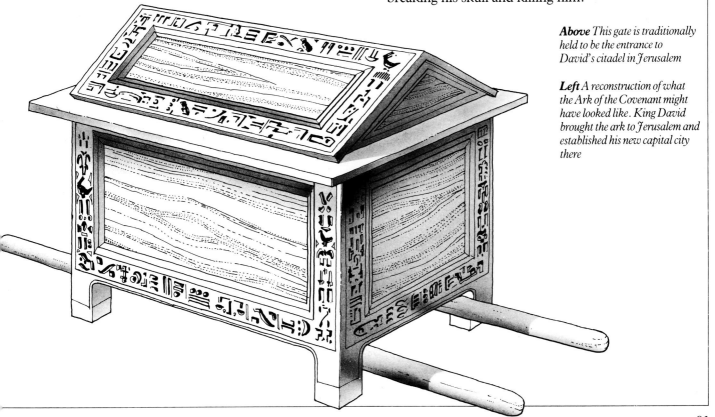

ABIGAIL

Meaning of name: Father of joy
Bible reference: 1 Sam. 25

A wife of **David**. Abigail was a beautiful and intelligent woman, married to a drunken, churlish man called Nabal. Nabal angered David by rudely refusing him and his men hospitality, but Abigail tactfully apologized for her husband and offered David generous provisions. Nabal had a stroke and died shortly after, and David married Abigail.

JOAB

Meaning of name: Jehovah is father
Bible reference: 2 Sam. 2:12–32, 3:22–31, 10–11, 14, 18, 19:1–8, 20, 24:1–4; 1 Kgs. 1:7, 19, 2:5–6, 22, 28–34; 1 Chron. 11:6, 8

David's nephew, and captain of his army. An ambitious and able man, Joab rose to become commander-in-chief over Israel. When David's captain Abner reluctantly killed Joab's brother in self-defense, Joab avenged him by murdering Abner. He understood David well, conniving with him in the affair of **Uriah** (*see* **Uriah**), and acting as peacemaker between David and **Absalom**, although it was Joab who was eventually responsible for Absalom's death (*see* **Absalom**). After this David appointed Amasa as commander, but Joab killed Amasa and was reinstated. However, David bore Joab grudges for these murders; before he died he told **Solomon** to avenge them, and Solomon had Joab killed.

ABSALOM

Meaning of name: Father of peace
Bible reference: 2 Sam. 3:3, 13–18

Third son of **David**. He was a handsome, charming young man and his father's favorite and heir. His half-brother Amnon fell in love with Absalom's sister Tamar and, after tricking her into visiting him at his house, raped her. Absalom arranged for Amnon to be killed, and then fled. David forgave him but Absalom plotted against his father and organized a rebellion against him. Pursued by his father's men, Absalom got caught by his long hair in an oak tree and was killed by David's captain, **Joab**, and his followers. When David heard of his death he wept, crying, "O my son Absalom, my son, my son Absalom! Would God I had died for thee, O Absalom, my son, my son!"

BATHSHEBA

Meaning of name: Seventh daughter
Bible reference: 2 Sam. 11–12:24; 1 Kgs. 1:11–31, 2:13–22

A wife of **David**. Bathsheba was a beautiful woman married to **Uriah**, one of David's soldiers. When David saw her bathing, he was attracted to her and sent for her to come to him. Bathsheba slept with the king and, when she later told him she had become pregnant, David had Uriah killed (*see* **Uriah**). Bathsheba married David but the son born to them died. Their second son was **Solomon**; when David was an old man, Bathsheba persuaded him to choose Solomon to succeed him.

URIAH

Meaning of name: Jehovah is light
Bible reference: 2 Sam. 11–12: 15, 23:39; 1 Kgs. 15:5

Husband of **Bathsheba**. Uriah the Hittite was one of **David**'s generals. When Bathsheba became pregnant (*see* **Bathsheba**), David sent for Uriah and encouraged him to go home, hoping that he would sleep with his wife and that the pregnancy could be attributed to him. When this ploy failed, David sent Uriah with a letter to **Joab** telling him to put Uriah in the forefront of the battle and leave him defenseless. Joab obeyed and Uriah was killed. The prophet Nathan opened David's eyes to the wickedness of this deed and he repented of it.

SOLOMON

Meaning of name: Peaceable
Bible reference: 2 Sam. 5:14, 1 Kgs. 1:10–53, 2–11; Neh. 13:26; Prov. 1:1

Son of **David** and **Bathsheba**, and king of Israel. After Solomon had succeeded David as king, God appeared to him in a dream and told him to ask for any gift. Solomon chose wisdom and God promised him not only wisdom but riches and honor. Solomon's finest act was the building of the temple in **Jerusalem**. Though he achieved great things in his forty-year reign, Solomon finally turned away from God. He had an enormous harem of foreign wives and concubines and they led him into idolatrous worship.

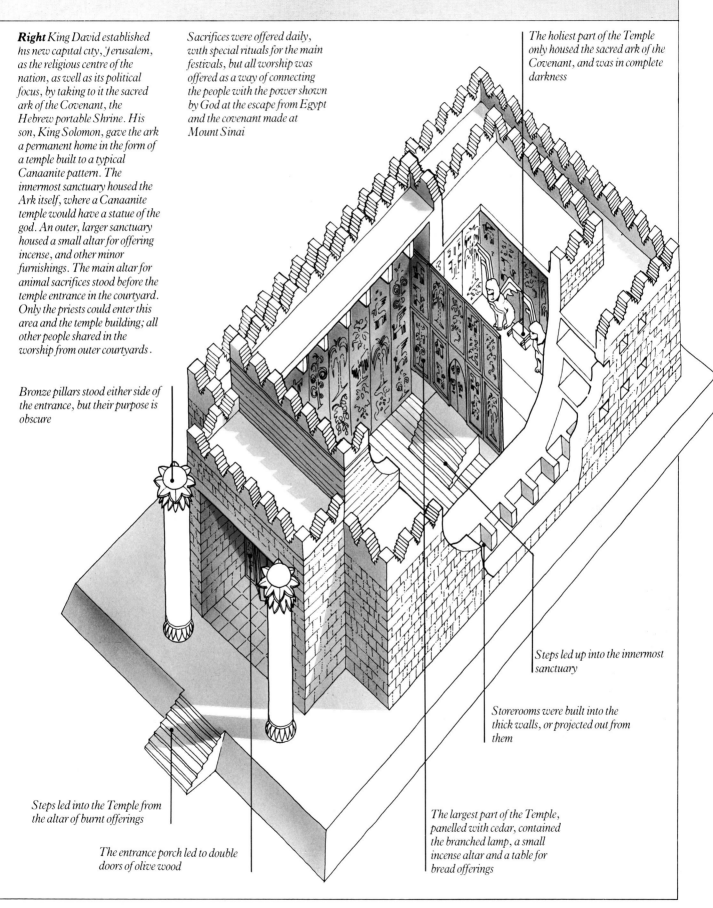

Right King David established his new capital city, Jerusalem, as the religious centre of the nation, as well as its political focus, by taking to it the sacred ark of the Covenant, the Hebrew portable Shrine. His son, King Solomon, gave the ark a permanent home in the form of a temple built to a typical Canaanite pattern. The innermost sanctuary housed the Ark itself, where a Canaanite temple would have a statue of the god. An outer, larger sanctuary housed a small altar for offering incense, and other minor furnishings. The main altar for animal sacrifices stood before the temple entrance in the courtyard. Only the priests could enter this area and the temple building; all other people shared in the worship from outer courtyards.

Bronze pillars stood either side of the entrance, but their purpose is obscure

Sacrifices were offered daily, with special rituals for the main festivals, but all worship was offered as a way of connecting the people with the power shown by God at the escape from Egypt and the covenant made at Mount Sinai

The holiest part of the Temple only housed the sacred ark of the Covenant, and was in complete darkness

Steps led up into the innermost sanctuary

Storerooms were built into the thick walls, or projected out from them

Steps led into the Temple from the altar of burnt offerings

The entrance porch led to double doors of olive wood

The largest part of the Temple, panelled with cedar, contained the branched lamp, a small incense altar and a table for bread offerings

CRIME IN THE BIBLE

In Old Testament times there was no distinction between civil and criminal law, and little distinction between the ideas of sin and of crime. The law was laid down by God, and punishment for breaking it was decreed by him. God is regarded in both the Old and New Testaments as the supreme judge.

The Woman Taken in Adultery *by Guercino (1591–1665) illustrates the story in John 8, where Jesus challenges the woman's accusers by saying, "He that is without sin among you, let him first cast a stone at her"*

SEXUAL OFFENCES

Leviticus 18 and 20 list various sexual offences for which death was the penalty: adultery, incest, homosexual intercourse, bestiality. Rape, however, was considered more of a property offence, and the penalty was reckoned in terms of the woman's bride price (e.g. Ex. 22:16–17). There is no condemnation of ordinary prostitution in the Old Testament, although ritual prostitution connected with idolatrous cults was abhorred.

Before the law was given to Moses, incest does not appear to have been considered an offence. **Sarah** was **Abraham**'s half-sister (Gen. 20:12); **Lot**'s daughters were not apparently punished for their incest with their father (Gen. 19:30–36). Rape seems to have been taken more seriously than the letter of the law suggests, especially if committed by strangers. Just as

Simeon and Levi revenged the rape of their sister Dinah by killing the Shechemites (Gen. 34), the men of Israel went to war against the Benjaminites to avenge the gang rape which had killed a Levite's concubine (Judg. 19–20). The rape of Tamar, **David**'s daughter, by her half-brother Amnon went unpunished at the time, but was avenged two years later by her brother **Absalom** (2 Sam. 13). Adultery was originally a capital offence, but by New Testament times it was so common that the penalty was rarely exacted. The Pharisees who presented Jesus with the woman taken in adultery (John 8:1–11) were hoping to trick him into denying the law.

BLASPHEMY

The punishment for blasphemy against God was death by stoning (Lev. 24:16). **Jezebel** had Naboth falsely accused of blasphemy and stoned to death (1 Kgs. 21:9–13). The accusation against Jesus was blasphemy (Mark 14:64) and he was killed by crucifixion only because he was handed over to the Roman authorities. Had the Jewish leaders punished him themselves, he would have been executed by stoning, as happened to **Stephen**, who was accused of the same crime (Acts 6:11, 7:58).

MURDER

The taking of life was regarded as the most serious offence, and it was normally punishable by death (Ex. 21:12). However, God's punishment for murder is not always death. The first murderer, **Cain**, was sentenced to exile rather than death (Gen. 5:8–15). The killing of a legitimate enemy, even if not actually in wartime, does not seem to count as murder. **Moses**' killing of the Egyptian (Ex. 1:11–12) was not held against him. Jael's murder of Sisera was a matter for high praise (Judg. 4:17–22, 5:24–31). **Jehu** had every member of the dynasty of **Ahab** killed (2 Kgs. 9–10) and God praised him for it (2 Kgs. 10:30). Genocide directed against God's own people was a different matter. Haman, in the book of Esther, attempted to destroy the whole Jewish nation and was hanged. **Herod the Great** is held in abhorrence for having all the infant boys in and around **Bethlehem** murdered (Matt. 2:16), although he apparently died a natural death afterwards.

THEFT

The first act of theft in the Bible is **Rachel**'s theft of her father's household gods (Gen. 31:19–35), which **Jacob** considered a crime worthy of death (v.32), although his wife was never punished for the offence. The story of **Joseph**

The first murder, when Cain killed his brother Abel, was caused by jealousy. This stained glass representation shows the brothers bringing their sacrifices to God

restoring the money with which his brothers had bought corn, and then planting his gold cup on them, suggests that thieves could be forced to serve their victims, at least in Egypt (Gen. 43:18, 44:17). After the law was given, theft was normally punished by exacting restitution of goods or a fixed compensation to the victim (e.g. Ex. 22:1). In an incident recorded in Judges 17:1–4, where a man admitted to stealing money from his mother, she appeared satisfied with restoration of the exact amount. However, theft in disobedience of a specific command of God was a much more serious offence. Achan, who stole war booty when God had forbidden this, was stoned to death with his family (Josh. 7). In Roman law, thieves were executed by crucifixion (Mark 15:27).

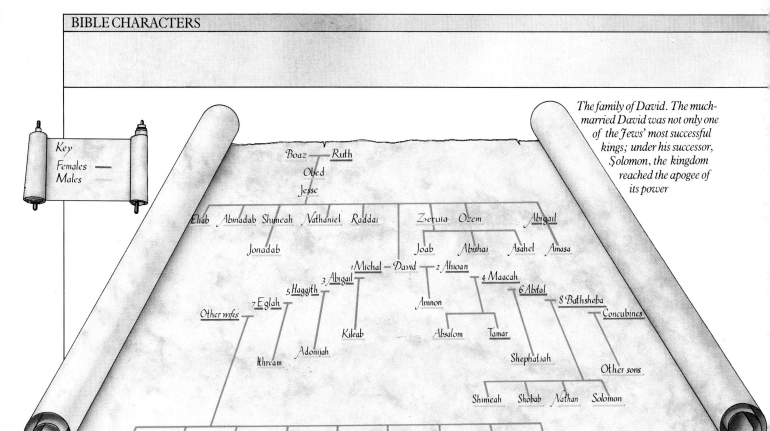

Key
Females —
Males —

The family of David. The much-married David was not only one of the Jews' most successful kings; under his successor, Solomon, the kingdom reached the apogee of its power

AHAB

Meaning of name: Father's brother
Bible reference: 1 Kgs. 16:28–33, 18:1–19:1, 20:
2–22:40

Seventh king of Israel. He was a successful warrior but, under the influence of his wife **Jezebel**, he introduced idolatry into the kingdom. Under his reign God's prophets were persecuted and worship of Baal was encouraged. Ahab's greed and disregard for justice are illustrated in the story of Naboth's vineyard (*see* **Jezebel**).

JEZEBEL

Meaning of name: Chaste
Bible reference: 1 Kgs. 16:31, 19:1–2, 21:1–25;
2 Kgs. 9:7–10, 30–37

Wife of **Ahab**. A worshiper of Baal and Asherah, she encouraged their worship in Israel, and was furious when **Elijah** killed the prophets of Baal (*see* **Elijah**). Ahab became depressed because he coveted a vineyard belonging to a man called Naboth who had refused to sell it to him. Jezebel arranged to have Naboth falsely accused of cursing God and the king, and he was stoned to death. Ahab then took possession of the vineyard but was denounced by Elijah. Elijah prophesied a horrible death for Jezebel and the prophesy was fulfilled by Jehu (*see* **Jehu**).

ELIJAH

Meaning of name: Jehovah is God
Bible reference: 1 Kgs. 17-19, 21; 2 Kgs. 1–2:15;
Mal. 4:5

Prophet during the reign of **Ahab**. Elijah was notable for his fearlessness in speaking to the king (*see* **Jezebel**) and for several miracles. Among these were the raising of the widow's son and the relief of the drought in Israel which had lasted three years. In this dramatic incident Elijah challenged the prophets of Baal on **Mount Carmel** to see whose god could answer their prayers with fire. When Baal had failed, Elijah built an altar and placed a sacrifice on it, soaking it in water, and God sent fire to consume it. Elijah then killed the prophets of Baal, and the same evening the rains came.

Elijah did not die but was taken up into heaven in a whirlwind.

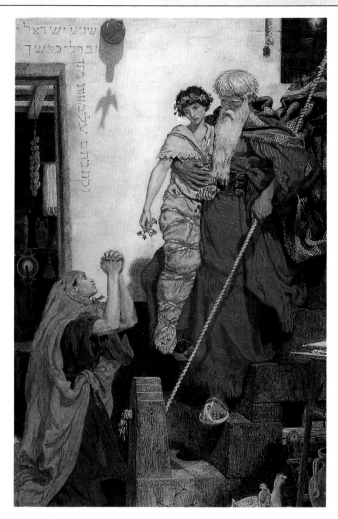

of the window, where she was smashed to pieces and trodden underfoot. Jehu continued to slay every remaining member of Ahab's family. He also killed all the worshipers of Baal and burned every image of the god, but he was not a sincere follower of God for he did nothing to stop the worship of golden calves.

NEBUCHADNEZZAR

Meaning of name: Nebo (*a Babylonian god*) protect the boundary
Bible reference: 2 Kgs. 24-25; Jer. 21:2,7; Ezek. 26:7, 29:18-19; Dan. 1–4

King of **Babylon**. A powerful ruler and military leader, Nebuchadnezzar conquered many nations. He captured Jerusalem, destroying the temple and taking captives back to Babylon. He promoted **Daniel** for interpreting his dreams, but continued in wickedness and idolatry. His pride was punished by a seven-year fit of madness, when he was driven out from the people and lived like an animal, eating grass. When he recovered, Nebuchadnezzar repented and praised God. (*See also* **Daniel**, **Shadrach**.)

ELISHA

Meaning of name: God is salvation
Bible reference: 1 Kgs. 19:16-21; 2 Kgs. 2:1–9:3, 13:14–21

Prophet of Israel. He served under **Elijah**, and inherited his ministry when Elijah was taken up to heaven. Though he was less fiery as a prophet than his predecessor, Elisha's ministry was also marked by miracles, including healings and raising from the dead. He was a prophet for fifty years.

JEHU

Meaning of name: Jehovah is he
Bible reference: 2 Kgs. 9–10

King of Israel. He was anointed by Elisha to replace **Ahab** as king. His first action was to drive furiously in his chariot to seek out Ahab's son Joram, king of **Judah**, and kill him, and then to have Ahab's wife **Jezebel** killed by ordering her servants to throw her out

Above left Elijah Raising the Widow's Son from the Dead *by Ford Madox Brown (1841–93) illustrates one of the great miracles performed by the prophet, and described in 1 Kgs 17*

Above Nebuchadnezzar *by William Blake (1757–1838) shows the great Assyrian king during the period when he was struck by madness as a punishment from God*

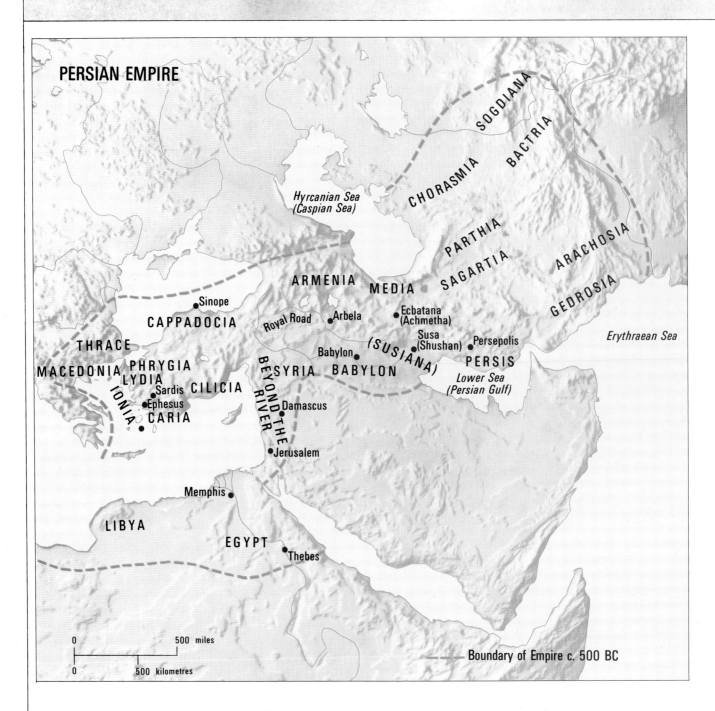

PERSIAN EMPIRE

Hyrcanian Sea
(Caspian Sea)

SOGDIANA

CHORASMIA

BACTRIA

PARTHIA

ARMENIA   MEDIA   SAGARTIA

ARACHOSIA

GEDROSIA

Sinope

CAPPADOCIA   Royal Road   •Arbela   •Ecbatana
(Achmetha)

Erythraean Sea

THRACE   •Susa
(Shushan)   •Persepolis

MACEDONIA   PHRYGIA   Babylon•   (SUSIANA)

LYDIA   •SYRIA   BABYLON   PERSIS

IONIA   •Sardis   CILICIA   BEYOND THE RIVER   Lower Sea
(Persian Gulf)

•Ephesus

CARIA   •Damascus

•Jerusalem

Memphis•

LIBYA

EGYPT

•Thebes

| 0 | | 500 miles |

| 0 | | 500 kilometres |

Boundary of Empire c. 500 BC

The extent of the Persian Empire and the surrounding regions at the time when the events of the book of Esther occurred

AHASUERUS

Meaning of name: King *or* mighty man
Bible reference: Esth. 1–10

Persian king, almost certainly identical with Xerxes I. He deposed his queen, Vashti, when she refused to appear to display her beauty to his drunken friends. He then married **Esther**, not knowing that she was Jewish. Urged on by Haman, his chief minister, Ahasuerus planned to destroy all the Jewish people in his kingdom. This plan was averted (*see* **Esther**), but Ahasuerus' change of heart and punishment of Haman indicate the capriciousness of his character rather than genuine repentance.

ESTHER

Meaning of name: Star
Bible reference: Esth. 1–10

A Jewish woman who became queen of Persia. She was an orphan and was brought up by her cousin Mordecai. When King Ahasuerus was looking for a new wife (*see* **Ahasuerus**), Mordecai entered Esther for what was virtually a beauty contest to select a queen. Esther was married to Ahasuerus but continued to accept Mordecai's advice.

Mordecai attracted the enmity of the king's chief minister, Haman, by refusing to bow to him, which led Haman to obtain the king's permission to order the destruction of all the Jews. Haman prepared a gallows upon which to hang Mordecai, but the king discovered that Mordecai had once been responsible for averting an assassination plot against him, so he had Mordecai publicly honored. Esther organized a banquet for the king and Ahasuerus told her to ask him for anything she wanted. She then interceded for her people and begged the king to stop the massacre. Haman was hanged on the gallows he had prepared for Mordecai but the royal proclamation against the Jews had already gone out. Ahasuerus allowed Esther and Mordecai to send out letters with the royal seal, warning the Jews to defend themselves. Having prepared and armed themselves, the Jews were able to kill their enemies.

JOB

Meaning of name: Pious, afflicted
Bible reference: Job 1–42

A man living in Uz. Job was an upright, godly, and prosperous man. God allowed Satan to test Job's faith and he was visited with various disasters, losing his ten children and his property and finally being struck down by a dreadful disease. Despite his suffering and the unhelpful advice of his wife and friends, Job remained faithful to God. Eventually his health and wealth were restored and he had ten more children.

Left Esther and Ahasuerus *by Francois Langrenee (1724–1805) showing Queen Esther presenting the king with her petition at the banquet she gave for him*

Above *An illustration from a twelfth-century manuscript showing Job scratching his sores. The figures on the right are Job's friends, whose unhelpful advice has led to the phrase "Job's comforters"*

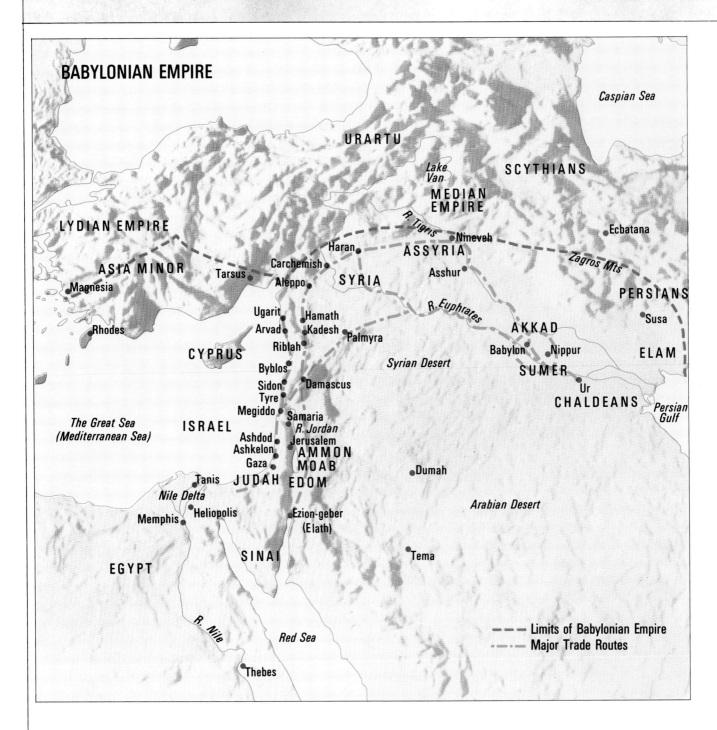

BABYLONIAN EMPIRE

Caspian Sea

URARTU

Lake Van

SCYTHIANS

MEDIAN EMPIRE

LYDIAN EMPIRE

Ecbatana

R. Tigris

Nineveh

ASSYRIA

Zagros Mts

ASIA MINOR

Haran

Carchemish

Asshur

PERSIANS

Magnesia

Tarsus

Aleppo

SYRIA

R. Euphrates

Susa

Rhodes

Ugarit

Hamath

AKKAD

ELAM

Arvad

Kadesh

Palmyra

Babylon

Nippur

Riblah

CYPRUS

Byblos

Damascus

Syrian Desert

SUMER

Ur

CHALDEANS

Persian Gulf

Sidon

Tyre

Megiddo

Samaria

The Great Sea (Mediterranean Sea)

ISRAEL

R. Jordan

Ashdod

Jerusalem

Ashkelon

AMMON

Gaza

MOAB

Tanis

JUDAH

EDOM

Dumah

Nile Delta

Memphis

Heliopolis

Ezion-geber (Elath)

Arabian Desert

SINAI

Tema

EGYPT

R. Nile

Red Sea

– – – Limits of Babylonian Empire

– · – · Major Trade Routes

Thebes

DANIEL

Meaning of name: God is my judge
Bible reference: Dan. 1–12

One of the major prophets. Of noble descent, Daniel was taken as a captive to **Babylon** and trained in the king's service. He gained prominence as a scholar and an interpreter of dreams, but persisted in his adherence to the Jewish religion. Having interpreted the dreams and visions of **Nebuchadnezzar** and **Belshazzar**, Daniel was promoted to the highest office under the next king, Darius. Other officials denounced Daniel to the king for praying to God, and Daniel was cast into a den of lions. When the lions did not harm the prophet, Darius decreed that Daniel's accusers should be thrown to the lions and that Daniel's God should be worshiped throughout the empire. (*See also* **Belshazzar**, **Nebuchadnezzar, Shadrach**.)

Left A map showing the extent of the Babylonian empire at the time of Daniel's captivity

Above Daniel was cast into a den of lions by the Babylonian king, Darius, but escaped unhurt. This ninth-century Irish carving depicts a very stylized representation of the scene in the lions' den

Below Belshazzar's Feast by Rembrandt (1606–69) showing the Babylonian king at the moment when the mysterious writing appears on the wall (Dan. 5)

SHADRACH

Meaning of name: Command of Aku (*moon god*)
Bible reference: Dan. 1:7, 2:49, 3

Companion of **Daniel**. When Daniel was taken into **Babylon**, three other Jewish youths were taken with him, Hananiah, Mishael, and Azariah, who were given the Babylonian names of Shadrach, Meshach, and Abednego. They found favor with **Nebuchadnezzar** because of their wisdom, and were given high office. But the king made a gold image and ordered everyone to worship it. Shadrach, Meshach, and Abednego refused to bow down to the image, and Nebuchadnezzar threatened to throw them into a fiery furnace if they persisted in their disobedience. They remained resolute and were thrown into the furnace, but were totally unscathed. The king praised their God and promoted the three men.

MESHACH

Meaning of name: Agile
Bible reference: Dan. 1:7, 2:49, 3

See **Shadrach**

ABEDNEGO

Meaning of name: Servant of light
Bible reference: Dan. 1:7, 2:49, 3

See **Shadrach**

BELSHAZZAR

Meaning of name: Bel protect the king
Bible reference: Dan. 5

King of **Babylon**. Belshazzar gave a great feast for a thousand of his lords. He took precious vessels belonging to God's temple and used them for the wine with which they toasted false gods. Suddenly a hand appeared and wrote on the wall of the palace the words MENE, MENE, TEKEL, UPHARSIN. The king was terrified and offered rich rewards to anyone who could interpret this mysterious writing. **Daniel** was brought in; he rebuked Belshazzar for his ungodly conduct, telling him that the message on the wall meant that his kingdom was doomed. That same night Belshazzar was killed.

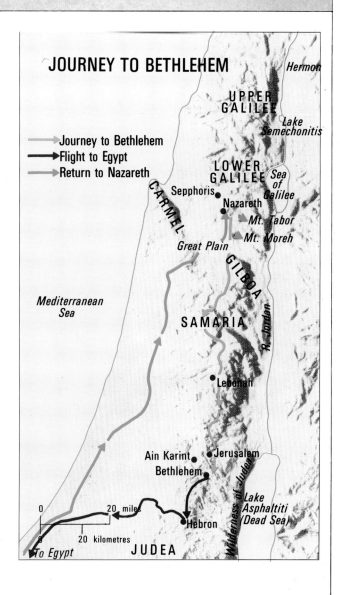

JOURNEY TO BETHLEHEM

→ Journey to Bethlehem
→ Flight to Egypt
→ Return to Nazareth

JONAH

Meaning of name: Dove
Bible reference: 2 Kgs. 14:25; Jon. 1–4

A minor prophet. God told Jonah to go to **Nineveh** and denounce the people's wickedness, but Jonah was afraid to do this and boarded a ship going to Tarshish instead. There was a tempest and the ship was in danger. Jonah admitted that he must be the cause, because he was trying to escape from God, so he was thrown overboard by the crew. He was swallowed by a large fish and remained in its belly for three days. After the fish vomited him out, Jonah obeyed God and preached to the people of Nineveh, who repented and were spared from punishment. Jonah resented God's mercy to them, but God taught him the need for compassion.

MARY

Meaning of name: Beloved *or* bitter
Bible reference: Matt. 1:18–24, 2:11, 12:46–47, 13:55; Luke 1:26–56, 2; John 2:1–12, 19:25; Acts 1:14

Mother of Jesus. An obscure young woman, living in **Nazareth**, Mary was betrothed to **Joseph** when the angel Gabriel visited her. She was told that she had found favor with God and would bear a child by the Holy Ghost. Mary humbly accepted this extraordinary situation, and eventually gave birth to Jesus in a stable in **Bethlehem**. Mary knew, from the circumstances of his birth, the visits of the shepherds and wise men, and the prayers of **Simeon** and **Anna**, whom Jesus was. It was she who encouraged him to perform his first miracle at **Cana**. After Jesus left home to begin his ministry, Mary rarely appears, but she was at the foot of the cross, and continued to meet with the disciples after Jesus' death and Resurrection. (*See also* **Joseph**, **John**, **Simeon**, **Anna**.)

JOSEPH, HUSBAND OF MARY

Meaning of name: God increases
Bible reference: Matt. 1: 18–25, 2:13–15, 19–23; Luke 2:4–5

Husband of **Mary**, mother of Jesus. Joseph was a carpenter, betrothed to Mary when she became pregnant. An angel told him in a dream that Mary's child was "conceived of the Holy Ghost," and would be the Savior, so Joseph married her; she subsequently gave birth to Jesus. In another dream Joseph was warned to escape **Herod the Great**'s wrath by fleeing to **Egypt**, and after Herod's death another angelic visitation brought him back to Israel, where he settled with his family in **Nazareth**. Joseph acted as a father to Jesus, but was apparently dead before Jesus' ministry began.

The Old Testament book most often quoted in the New Testament is Isaiah, with 419 references, followed by the book of Psalms which is referred to 414 times.

ELISABETH

Meaning of name: God is my oath
Bible reference: Luke 1:5–7, 24–26, 36, 39–45, 57–61

Mother of **John the Baptist**. She was a pious woman from a priestly family and was married to a priest, **Zacharias**. They were old and childless, but after her husband had a vision (*see* **Zacharias**) Elisabeth became pregnant. When **Mary**, who was a relation of Elisabeth's, came to her house, the baby leapt in Elisabeth's womb. Filled with the Holy Spirit, she said to Mary, "Blessed art thou among women, and blessed is the fruit of thy womb." Mary stayed at the house for three months, and then Elisabeth gave birth to the son who was to become John the Baptist.

ZACHARIAS

Meaning of name: Jehovah is renowned
Bible reference: Luke 1:5–24, 57–79

Father of **John the Baptist**. Zacharias was a priest and he and his wife **Elisabeth** were godly people, but childless. The angel Gabriel appeared to Zacharias in his old age and told him that Elisabeth would have a son, who must be called John, and who would be a great man of God. Zacharias could not believe that he and Elisabeth could have children at their age. Gabriel said that, because of his disbelief, Zacharias would be struck dumb until the prophesy was fulfilled. When John was born it was assumed that he would be named after his father, but Zacharias wrote down, "His name is John." Then at once his dumbness left him and he praised God and prophesied about John's mission.

SIMEON

Meaning of name: Hearing
Bible reference: Luke 2: 25–35

A devout man of **Jerusalem**. God had told Simeon that he would not die before he had seen the Messiah. He was in the temple in Jerusalem when **Mary** and **Joseph** brought Jesus to present him to God. Simeon took the baby in his arms and praised God, saying that now he had seen Jesus he was happy to die. He prophesied that Jesus would be a light to the Gentiles and a glory to Israel. (*See also* **Anna**.)

ANNA

Meaning of name: Grace
Bible reference: Luke 2:36–38

A prophetess, Anna was an old woman who had been widowed for many years. She spent her time in the temple in **Jerusalem**, fasting and praying, waiting for the Messiah to come. When **Mary** and **Joseph** brought Jesus to the temple, Anna recognized the baby as the Messiah, and gave thanks to God. She subsequently spoke of the child to all those who, like her, were waiting for God's redemption. (*See also* **Simeon**.)

HEROD THE GREAT

Meaning of name: Son of the hero
Bible reference: Matt. 2

King at the time of Jesus' birth. When his wise men announced the birth of a king in **Bethlehem** he sent them to search for the child. When they failed to return, Herod ordered the slaughter of all the children under the age of two in the Bethlehem region.

JOHN THE BAPTIST

Meaning of name: God is gracious
Bible reference: Matt. 3, 11:2–19, 21:25–32; Mark 6:14–29; Luke 1:5–25, 57–80, 7:18–33; John 3:23–30

Prophet and preacher. Born to the elderly **Elisabeth** and **Zacharias**, he grew up in the desert and lived an ascetic life. He was a fiery preacher and gained fame for his message, which centered upon the need for people to repent of their sins and be baptized. He baptized many people in the Jordan, including Jesus himself. John recognized that he was the forerunner of a greater one, preparing the way for Jesus. His forthright preaching made him many enemies and he was eventually beheaded (*see* **Salome**).

Although there were established Jewish cleansing rituals John's baptism was the first to be directly linked with the idea of repentance, and is the origin of Christian baptism. This picture of John baptizing Jesus in the River Jordan is part of an altarpiece by Piero della Francesca (c. 1416–92)

ANGELS IN THE BIBLE

Angels in the Bible are spiritual beings of a higher order than humans. They have a close relationship with God, seeing him face to face, and usually act as messengers from him. Cherubim and seraphim are higher orders of angelic beings, and were thought to be winged creatures who guarded the throne of God.

ANGELS IN THE OLD TESTAMENT

The first angels to be mentioned in the Bible are the cherubim who were placed on guard at the garden of Eden (Gen. 3:24). The Bible does not say in what form the angel of the Lord appeared to **Hagar** (Gen. 16:7–11), but the angels whom **Abraham** entertained (Gen. 18:2–16) and those who rescued **Lot** from **Sodom** (Gen. 19:1–16) apparently appeared in the guise of ordinary men.

When the expression "the angel of the Lord" is used, the angel always acts as God's mouthpiece and is virtually identified with God (e.g. Gen. 22:11, 31:11–13; Ex. 3:2). The term "sons of God" (e.g. Job 1:6) is just another name for angels.

Although angels are most often messengers, they can also bring material help to mortals (e.g. 1 Kgs. 19:5–7, where an angel provides food for **Elijah**) and give

Top The Annunciation *by Leonardo da Vinci (1452–1519) shows the angel Gabriel with the Virgin Mary.* ***Above*** *This Italian fresco shows the three angels that were entertained by Abraham.* ***Right*** *A fifteenth-century painted stone representation of an angel from Burgundy*

aid in battle (e.g. 2 Kgs. 19:35). Angels often appear in visions (e.g. Is. 6:1–7; Zech. 1:8ff). It is in the book of Daniel that angels are first given names: Gabriel and Michael.

ANGELS IN THE NEW TESTAMENT

The angel Gabriel appears both to **Zacharias** and to **Mary** to announce the coming births of **John the Baptist** and Jesus (Luke 1:5–38), while the angel of the Lord appears three times to **Joseph** (Matt. 1:20, 2:13,19). Elsewhere in the Gospels, angels minister to Jesus (Matt. 4:11; Luke 24:43), and he speaks of them often in association with the final judgment (e.g. Matt. 16:27; Mark 8:38). The angel who rolled away the stone from Jesus' tomb had a "countenance … like lightning and … raiment white as snow" (Matt. 28:3).

Angels feature several times in the book of Acts: for example, releasing **Peter** from prison (12:1–19) and giving information and instructions to **Paul** and **Philip** (8:26, 27:23–24). However, it is in the book of Revelation that angels are mentioned most frequently. Here they are represented as active in the final battle against Satan (e.g. 12:7), and as pouring out the wrath of God upon the earth (15, 16).

DEVILS IN THE BIBLE

Satan, or the Devil, is God's adversary, the supreme spirit of evil. He is sometimes portrayed as the leader of an army of fallen angels, and sometimes as a subtle tempter of mortals. The idea of demons, or evil spirits, is mainly confined to the New Testament.

THE OLD TESTAMENT

The spirit of evil first appears in Genesis 3, in the form of the serpent that tempts **Eve** and brings about the expulsion from the garden of Eden. It is first referred to by name in 1 Chronicles 21, when Satan provokes **David** to number the people, contrary to God's will. Satan appears again in the story of **Job**, when he obtains permission to test Job's faith.

The idea of the Devil as Lucifer, the fallen angel cast from heaven

Before he began his ministry Jesus spent forty days praying and fasting in the wilderness, and the Devil tempted him there. This picture of Satan Watching the Sleep of Christ *is by Joseph Noel Paton (1821–1901)*

The Fall of the Rebel Angels *from the fourteenth-century* Très Riches Heures du Duc de Berry *illustrates the vision of John (Rev. 12:90) where Satan and all his angels were cast out of heaven*

because of his pride, derives from Isaiah 14:12–15. Although Isaiah was not actually referring to the Devil, but to the King of Babylon, the name Lucifer has become associated with Satan because of the similarity of passages such as Luke 10:18 and Revelation 9:1 to the Isaiah scripture.

When the word "devils" is used, it usually refers to alien deities (e.g. Lev. 17:7; Ps. 106:37), but the term "evil spirit" is used to describe the madness that afflicts **Saul** (1 Sam. 16:14).

THE NEW TESTAMENT

The New Testament refers frequently to the Devil, either by that name or as Satan, Beelzebub (e.g. Matt. 10:25), or titles such as "the prince of the power of the air" (Eph. 2:2). He is seen in the Gospels tempting Jesus (Matt. 4), attempting to work through **Peter** (Matt. 16:22–23; Luke 22:31), and causing **Judas** to betray Jesus (John 13:2). Satan is referred to in the letters of Paul, James, Peter, John, and Jude as an evil tempter against whom Christians must be perpetually vigilant.

The Gospels and book of Acts contain many stories about physical and mental afflictions caused by "demons" or "evil spirits." These appear to be spiritual beings under Satan's rule who cause suffering and confusion to humankind. Jesus cast out evil spirits responsible for a variety of disorders.

HEAVEN AND HELL IN THE BIBLE

Most of the traditional ideas that we have about heaven and hell derive from a few passages in the New Testament, which have been much elaborated by subsequent writers. Jewish ideas about the afterlife are very much less specific than Christian ones, and we cannot form any complete picture of Hebrew theology on heaven and hell from the Old Testament.

PARADISE

The word "paradise" comes from an Iranian word meaning a walled garden. When the Hebrew word is used in the Old Testament it is always used in this literal sense (e.g. Neh. 2:8). However, in Jewish thought, paradise became associated first with the garden of Eden, and then with the idea of a concealed heaven, resembling Eden, to which the souls of the righteous would be taken.

The Garden of Earthly Delights *by Hieronymous Bosch (c. 1450–1516) shows a somewhat unspiritual vision of Paradise*

This detail from the Last Judgment *by Rogier van der Weyden (1399–1464) portrays the wicked being led off into hell*

In the New Testament, the word is used in three different ways. Jesus tells the man crucified next to him, "Today shalt thou be with me in paradise" (Luke 23:43), suggesting the place to which souls go immediately after death. In 2 Corinthians 12:2–4, **Paul**, speaking of himself in the third person, describes a visionary experience of being caught up in the "third heaven," which he also calls "paradise." There may be some reference here to an idea in Jewish thought that there is a hierarchy of seven heavens. In Revelation 2:7, paradise is the place where the tree of life stands – another identification with Eden.

HEAVEN

In the Old Testament there is no real distinction between "heaven" and "the heavens." Heaven was the sky above, through which the rain fell (Gen. 7:11), and across which the sun passed (Ps. 19:4–6). It was also the abode of God and the angels (e.g. Deut. 26:15; Neh. 9:6). In the New Testament, too, while the word "heaven" is sometimes used synonymously for God (e.g. Luke 15:18 and also Matthew's use of "the kingdom of heaven"), there is an idea of a physical location above. Jesus "lifted up his eyes to heaven" to pray (John 17:1), and the disciples witnessed the Ascension – a physical raising of the resurrected Jesus up to heaven.

The idea of heaven as the ultimate destination for the

righteous is only found in the New Testament. Jesus tells the disciples that he is going to prepare a place for them there (John 14:2), and speaks of people sitting with the patriarchs in heaven (Matt. 8:11), and of the kingdom inherited by the righteous at the last judgment (Matt. 25:34). The thought that both heaven and earth will ultimately pass away to be replaced by a new heaven and new earth is found in the Old Testament (Is. 65:17), but is developed fully in the book of Revelation. The portrait of the new Jerusalem, with its gates of pearl, where God is enthroned and believers see him face to face (Rev. 21, 22), is the basis for the traditional Christian idea of heaven.

SHEOL

"Sheol" is a Hebrew word used for the abode of the dead. It is thought of as a place situated below the ground (e.g. Ekek. 31:15), a place of darkness, silence, and forgetfulness (Job 10:21; Ps. 94:17, 88:12). Although the dead in Sheol are apparently cut off from God (Ps. 88:3–5), he is not absent (Ps. 139:8), and is able to deliver souls from Sheol (Ps. 16:10). It is sometimes translated as "hell"; however, it is not seen as a place of eternal punishment, and its use in the New Testament (e.g. Matt. 16:18; Acts 2:27) suggests a meaning relating simply to the power of death.

HELL

The word translated as "hell" in the New Testament comes from the Hebrew word "Gehenna." Gehenna meant "the valley of Hinnom," and was originally a particular valley outside Jerusalem, where children were sacrificed to the god Moloch (2 Kgs. 23:10; 2 Chron. 28:3; Jer. 32:35). In later Jewish literature Gehenna came to be associated with a place of torment and unquenchable fire that was to be the punishment for sinners. It was thought by many that lesser sinners might eventually be delivered from the fires of Gehenna, but by New Testament times punishment for sinners was deemed to be eternal.

Jesus speaks of hell as a place of everlasting fire that was prepared for the Devil and his angels (Matt. 25:41) but is also the destination for those who fail to do God's will. Hell is described as the place where both body and soul are destroyed (Matt. 10:28) and where there is "weeping and gnashing of teeth" (Matt. 8:12); it is often associated with blackness and darkness (e.g. Matt. 22:13; 2 Pet. 2:17; Jude 13). The book of Revelation reinforces the idea of fire and brimstone (e.g. 21:8), but other New Testament passages emphasize the idea of eternal punishment as separation from Christ (e.g. Matt. 7:23; 2 Thess. 1:9).

ANDREW

Meaning of name: Manly
Bible reference: Matt. 4:18–20; Mark 13:3;
John 1:40–42, 44, 6:8–9, 12:22

One of the twelve apostles. He was a disciple of **John the Baptist**, who introduced him to Jesus. Andrew then brought his brother **Peter** to see Jesus, and they were later both called from their fishing boats to become disciples. It was Andrew who drew Jesus' attention to the boy with the five loaves and two fishes which fed the five thousand.

PETER (CEPHAS)

Meaning of name: Rock
Bible reference: Matt. 4:18–20, 8:14, 14:25–32,
16:13–23, 17:1–4, 26:31–40, 69–75; Luke 24:12;
John 13:6–9, 18:10–11, 20:2–6, 21:7–21; Acts 1:13,
2:14–40, 3:1–4: 23, 5:1–10, 15, 8:14–25, 9:32–12; 19,
15:7–11; Gal. 2:11–14; *see also* 1 Pet.; 2 Pet.

One of the twelve apostles. A fisherman, originally named Simon, Peter was called to discipleship with his brother **Andrew**. He was one of those closest to Jesus, and was a warm-hearted and impulsive man who often acted without thinking, as on the occasion when he tried to walk on water, or when he cut off the ear of the soldier who arrested Jesus. Despite his deep love for Jesus and commitment to him, Peter often failed to understand him, and his courage deserted him after Jesus' arrest when Peter denied knowledge of him three times.

　　After the Resurrection and the coming of the Holy Spirit, Peter became a true "rock" and the main leader of the Church. He became a bold preacher and a worker of miracles. Despite his vision that the gospel was for the Gentiles too (*see* **Cornelius**), Peter was later rebuked by **Paul** for refusing to eat with Gentiles.

JAMES THE APOSTLE

Meaning of name: Follower, supplanter
Bible reference: Matt. 4:21–22, 17:1; Mark 1:29, 5:37,
10:35–41, 13:3, 14:32–40; Luke 9:54; Acts 1:13, 12:2

One of the twelve apostles and son of Zebedee. A fisherman, James was called to be a disciple at the same time as his brother **John**. He witnessed the Transfiguration and was among the select few disciples closest to Jesus. He was put to death by **Herod Agrippa 1**.

JOHN

Meaning of name: God is gracious
Bible reference: Matt. 4:21–22, 17:1; Mark 1:29, 5:37,
10:35–41, 13:3, 14:32–40; Luke 9:49, 54, 22:8;
Acts 1:13, 3:1–11, 4:1–23, 8:14–25; Gal. 2:9

One of the twelve apostles. The son of Zebedee and brother of **James**, John was one of the disciples closest to Jesus. He is not mentioned by name in the Gospel of John, but is assumed to be "the disciple whom Jesus loved" (John 13:23, 19:26–27), to whom Jesus entrusted the care of his mother before he died. As a leader in the early Church, his name is usually linked with that of **Peter**.

Above Christ's Charge to Peter *attributed to Giuseppe Vermiglio (1586–1635) illustrates Matthew 16:18–19 where Jesus entrusts his Church* *to the apostle. The picture shows the symbols associated with Peter, a rock and the keys of heaven*

MATTHEW

Meaning of name: Gift of Jehovah
Bible reference: Matt. 9:9–10; Mark 3:18; Luke 5:27–29

One of the twelve apostles. He is assumed to be the same person as the disciple Levi mentioned in the Gospels of Mark and Luke. Matthew was a tax-collector, a despised occupation, and he was called by Jesus when sitting in the tax office. He then gave a feast for Jesus, who was criticized for eating with such people.

Above Although the Gospel of Matthew is now generally attributed to an unknown author, it was long thought to have been written by the apostle Matthew. The painting by Juan de Pareja (1610–70) is titled **The Vocation of St Matthew**

Right This picture of St John the Evangelist with his Gospel comes from a manuscript of John's Gospel. It is, in fact, unlikely that "the beloved apostle" actually wrote the fourth Gospel

> *He [the translator] will find one book and one only, where, as in the Iliad itself, perfect plainness of speech is allied with perfect nobleness; and that book is the Bible.*
>
> MATTHEW ARNOLD 1822–1888

BARTHOLOMEW

Meaning of name: Son of Talmai
Bible reference: Matt. 10:3

One of the twelve apostles. He is thought to be identical with **Nathanael** (*see* **Nathanael**).

NATHANAEL

Meaning of name: Gift of God
Bible reference: John 1:45–49, 21:2

One of the twelve apostles, thought to be the same person as **Bartholomew**. When **Philip** told him that he had found the Messiah, Nathanael doubted that a Galilean could be the promised one. However, when he saw Jesus, who appeared to know him although they had never met, Nathanael hailed him as the Son of God. Jesus described Nathanael as "an Israelite indeed in whom is no guile".

PHILIP THE APOSTLE

Meaning of name: Lover of horses
Bible reference: Matt. 10:3; John 1:43–48, 6:5–7, 12:21–22, 14:8–9

One of the twelve apostles. It was Philip who told **Nathanael** that he had found the Messiah. Jesus tested Philip by asking him how to feed the five thousand, but Philip failed to anticipate the miracle and answered in practical terms.

THOMAS

Meaning of name: Twin
Bible reference: Matt. 10:3; John 11:16, 14:5, 20:24–28, 21:2; Acts 1:13

One of the twelve apostles. When Jesus first appeared to his disciples after the Resurrection, Thomas was not with them. When they told him that they had seen the risen Jesus, Thomas said he would not believe it until he had himself touched the nail scars in Jesus' hands and the spear wound in his side. A week later Jesus appeared again and, when he saw Thomas, invited him to touch his hands and side. Thomas answered, "My Lord and my God."

SIMON THE APOSTLE

Meaning of name: Hearing
Bible reference: Matt. 10:4; Acts 1:13

One of the twelve apostles. He was known as Simon the zealot, presumably because of his patriotic fervour.

JUDAS

Meaning of name: Praise of the Lord
Bible reference: Matt. 10:4, 26:14–16, 20–25, 47–49, 27:3–10; John 6:70–71, 12:4–6; Acts 1:16–25

One of the twelve apostles. He was the treasurer, and apparently carried out this task dishonestly. Jesus said at the Last Supper that one of his disciples would betray him; Judas had in fact agreed to hand him over to the authorities in return for thirty pieces of silver. Judas identified Jesus to the soldiers who came to arrest him by kissing him. According to Matthew, Judas hanged himself after Jesus' arrest, but Acts says that he purchased a field with the silver and fell there, bursting open and spilling his bowels out.

HEROD ANTIPAS

Meaning of name: Son of the hero
Bible reference: Mark 6: 14–29; Luke 9: 7–9, 13:31, 23:6–12, 15

Son of **Herod the Great**. He had **John the Baptist** killed (*see* **Salome**), and delivered Jesus up to Pilate.

SALOME

Meaning of name: Peace
Bible reference: Mark 6: 19–28

Stepdaughter of **Herod Antipas**. **John the Baptist** had enraged Herodias, Herod's wife, by criticizing their marriage on the grounds that she was Herod's brother's wife. At Herodias' request, John was imprisoned. On Herod's birthday, Salome, Herodias' daughter, came in and danced for him. Her dancing pleased him so much that he said he would give her anything she asked for. She consulted her mother, who told her to ask for the head of John the Baptist. Salome demanded John's head on a charger, and Herod kept his promise.

There are two books in the Bible that never mention the name of God: the book of Esther and the Song of Solomon.

The most married man in the Bible is Solomon, who had seven hundred wives, not to mention three hundred concubines (1 Kgs. 11:3).

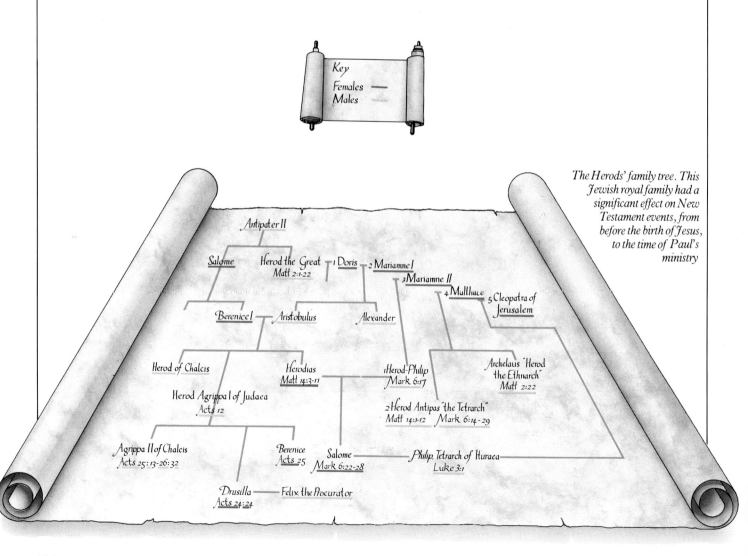

Key
Females ——
Males ——

The Herods' family tree. This Jewish royal family had a significant effect on New Testament events, from before the birth of Jesus, to the time of Paul's ministry

CLOTHES IN THE BIBLE

*According to Genesis 3, clothes only became necessary as a result of the
Fall, and thereafter in the Bible nakedness is associated with shame. There
are no very detailed accounts of dress in the Bible, but it is possible to gain
some ideas from contemporary Egyptian and Babylonian illustrations.*

The basic dress for Israelite men
was a sort of tunic made of wool or
linen, with or without sleeves, and
reaching to the knees or ankles. A
more elaborate version of this tunic
was sometimes worn, and was
likely to be highly colored.
Joseph's "coat of many colors"
(Gen. 37:3) was probably a tunic
with sleeves.

The ordinary mantle or cloak
worn over the tunic was a square
piece of cloth worn over one or
both shoulders and with holes for
the arms. It was used as a covering
at night (Ex. 22: 26–27), and for
carrying things (e.g. Judg. 8:25).
Other kinds of cloak were made of
animal skin and worn by prophets

*This Egyptian representation of Palestinian
merchants gives some idea of how Hebrew
people would dress around the time of Moses*

(e.g. Zech. 13:4; Matt. 3:4).
The headdress was usually a
cloth square worn as a protection
from the sun. The "bonnets" worn

by **Aaron**'s sons (Ex. 28:40) were
linen turbans. Poor people went
barefoot, but sandals with wooden
or leather soles were also worn,
mainly for traveling. They were
fastened with thongs or "latchets"
(King James Version, e.g. Gen.
14:23; Mark 1:7).

Women's clothing was very
similar to men's, but obviously not
completely identical, for there is a
prohibition on women wearing
men's clothes and vice versa in
Deuteronomy 10:5. Women's
clothes were likely to be of finer
material and more brightly colored
than men's, and veils were worn.

Priests always wore special
clothing, although the oldest
sacred dress seems to have been a
very simple white linen loincloth
("ephod" in the King James
Version) such as **David** wore to
dance before the Lord (2 Sam.
6:14). High priests wore a much
more elaborate and costly garment
of gold, purple, or scarlet (Ex.
39:1–29). Priests were not allowed
to wear wool (Ezek. 44:17).

Jewelry was highly prized, not
just for ornamentation but as a
form of wealth before coins were
introduced (2 Chron. 21:3).
Jewelry mentioned includes
earrings and bracelets (e.g. Gen.
26:22; Ezek. 16:11–12), necklaces
(e.g. Gen. 41:42), crowns (e.g. 2
Sam. 1:10), and rings for fingers
(e.g. Ex. 35:22; Luke 15:22).
Stones used were more likely to be
semi-precious than precious, but
gold and precious stones were
sometimes used.

*The Hebrew phrase
traditionally
translated as "coat
of many colors" is
obscure, and
Joseph's coat was
probably a coat with
long sleeves or a
richly decorated
robe. The picture*
The Coat of Many
Colors *is by Ford
Madox Brown
(1821-93)*

MARTHA

Meaning of name: Lady, mistress
Bible reference: Luke 10:38–42; John 11–12:2

Sister of **Mary** and **Lazarus**. Martha was the practical one of the two sisters. When she complained that her sister was not helping her with serving food, Jesus gently rebuked her for her fussing. Martha's faith in Jesus was absolute. When her brother died (*see* **Lazarus**) she was sure that Jesus would have been able to save him had he arrived in time, and she declared her belief in Jesus as the Son of God.

Right *Jesus' relationship with the family at Bethany shows his human side as a person with friends who were special and dear to him.* Christ in the House of Martha and Mary *by Jan Vermeer (1632–75) shows Mary, the contemplative sister, sitting at Christ's feet and listening to his teaching. Martha the practical sister, is busy serving food*

Far right *The miracle by which Martha and Mary's brother Lazarus was raised from the dead was the means of converting many people to belief in Jesus, but was also the main provocation for those seeking his death (John 11).* The Resurrection of Lazarus *is by Lambert Zutman (1510–67)*

MARY OF BETHANY

Meaning of name: Beloved *or* bitter
Bible reference: Luke 10: 38–42; John 11, 12:3–7

Sister of **Martha** and **Lazarus**. While her sister busied herself with housework, Mary chose to sit at Jesus' feet and listen to his teaching, and Jesus praised her for her choice. After the raising of Lazarus (*see* **Lazarus**) Jesus had supper with the family at **Bethany**. Mary took a jar of very expensive scented ointment and anointed Jesus' feet, wiping them with her hair. **Judas** criticized her action but Jesus defended her.

LAZARUS

Meaning of name: God is help
Bible reference: John 11, 12:1–17

Brother of **Martha** and **Mary**. This family, living at **Bethany**, were friends of Jesus. Lazarus became sick and his sisters asked Jesus to come to him. Jesus did not go straight away and, by the time he got to Bethany, Lazarus was dead and buried. Jesus wept with Lazarus' sisters at the grave, then asked them to take away the stone at the mouth of the cave where the body lay. He called "Lazarus, come forth," and Lazarus walked out alive.

ZACCHAEUS

Meaning of name: Jehovah is renowned
Bible reference: Luke 19: 1–10

A tax-collector of **Jericho**. Zacchaeus had become rich through fraudulent dealings as a tax-collector. When Jesus came to Jericho, Zacchaeus wanted to see him, but he was very short and could not see through the crowds, so he climbed a sycamore tree to get a better view. As Jesus passed he looked up and called to Zacchaeus to come down, for he was going to stay at his house. People were shocked that Jesus was to be the guest of such a sinner, but Zacchaeus told Jesus that he would repay all those he had cheated and give half his goods to the poor.

NICODEMUS

Meaning of name: Victor of the people
Bible reference: John 3:1–10, 7:50–51, 19:39

A Jewish leader. Nicodemus was a Pharisee who recognized by the miracles he saw that Jesus had come from God. He went to see Jesus by night, but was puzzled by his teaching that people need to be born again of the Spirit. He was subsequently brave enough to speak up for Jesus to the Pharisees, and he was one of those who brought spices to anoint Jesus' body after his death.

The longest psalm in the Bible is Psalm 119, which has 176 verses; the shortest is Psalm 117 with just two verses. The longest verse in the Bible (King James Version) is Esther 8:9, which runs to ninety words, and the shortest is John 11:35: "Jesus wept."

PILATE

Meaning of name: Armed with a dart
Bible reference: Matt. 27:1–26; Luke 3:1, 13:1; John 18:28–19:23, 19:38; Acts 4:27

Roman governor. Jesus was delivered into Pilate's hands after his arrest. Pilate was unwilling to interfere in Jewish religious affairs and could find no fault in Jesus. His wife also warned him not to be involved, because of a dream she had had. However, when his one attempt to release Jesus had failed (*see* **Barabbas**), Pilate washed his hands to demonstrate his own innocence and then ordered Jesus to be flogged and crucified.

BARABBAS

Meaning of name: Son of a father
Bible reference: Matt. 27:16–26

A man imprisoned for sedition and murder. At the time of the Passover, it was the custom to release any prisoner of the people's choice. **Pilate** hoped to release Jesus in this way, but the priests organized a popular movement in favor of Barabbas. When Pilate offered them the choice of releasing Jesus or Barabbas, the people clamored to have Barabbas released and Jesus crucified, and this was done.

MARY MAGDALENE

Meaning of name: Beloved *or* bitter
Bible reference: Matt. 27:56, 61, 28:1–10; Luke 8:2; John 20:1–2, 11–18

A follower of Jesus. She is said to have been healed by Jesus from a sickness caused by demon possession. She was with the other women at the foot of the cross and, according to John, was the first to see the resurrected Lord. She was weeping at the tomb when he appeared, and at first she mistook him for a gardener. Jesus spoke her name and she recognized him. He told her not to touch him, for he had not yet ascended to his Father, but to tell the other disciples what she had seen.

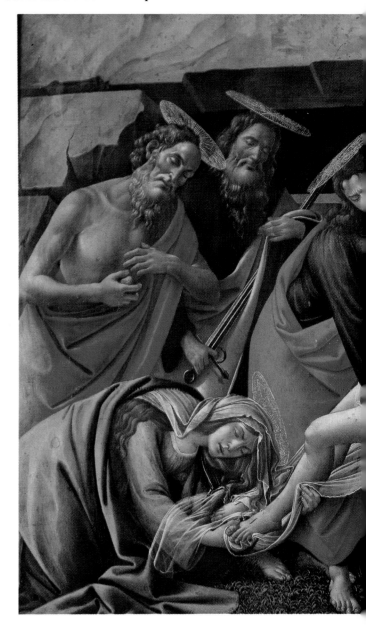

*In the twentieth century our highest praise has
been to call the Bible "the world's best-seller."
And it has come to be more and more difficult to
say whether we think it is a best-seller because it
is great, or vice versa.*

DANIEL BOORSTIN 1914–

Left *Mary Magdalene is
sometimes identified with the
unnamed sinful woman in Luke
7:37–48, particularly as her
home town Magdala was
apparently famous for
immorality. In this Pietà by
Botticelli (1440–1510) Mary
Magdalene is cradling the head
of the crucified Christ*

Far left *As governor of the
Roman province of Judaea,
Pontius Pilate was responsible
for the trial of Jesus under
Roman law. This representation
of Christ before Pilate comes
from a fourth-century marble
sarcophagus*

JAMES

Meaning of name: Follower, supplanter
Bible reference: Matt. 13:55; Acts 12:17, 15:13–21, 1 Cor. 15:7, Gal. 1:19, 2:9,12

Brother of Jesus. There is no evidence that James was a believer in his brother's lifetime, but Jesus appeared to him after the Resurrection and James became a prominent leader in the early Church.

BARNABAS

Meaning of name: Son of exhortation
Bible reference: Acts 4:36–37, 11:22–30, 12:25, 13–15; 1 Cor. 9–6; Gal. 2:1, 9, 13; Col. 4:10

Apostle and missionary. He had a close relationship with **Paul** and accompanied him on many of his missionary journeys. Having been a believer before Paul's conversion, Barnabas originally took the lead in the partnership, but Paul later became dominant. Barnabas was a good man and a dedicated missionary but was not strong enough in character to withstand pressures from the Jewish Christians who were refusing to eat with Gentile believers. Barnabas was apparently impressive enough in appearance for the Lycaonians to mistake him for the god Jupiter.

PHILIP THE EVANGELIST

Meaning of name: Lover of horses
Bible reference: Acts 6:5, 8:5–40, 21:8–9

Deacon and evangelist. He was an effective preacher, responsible for many conversions, including those of **Simon the magician** and the Ethiopian eunuch, whom Philip baptized right away as they were traveling close to water.

STEPHEN

Meaning of name: Crown
Bible reference: Acts: 6:5, 8–15, 7, 8:2

Deacon and first Christian martyr. Stephen is described as a man "full of faith and of the Holy Ghost." His preaching and miracles brought him to the attention of certain zealous Jews who had him accused of blasphemy. Stephen defended himself by preaching on the history of Israel and the people's constant rejection of God's prophets and finally of the Messiah. This infuriated the council, and when Stephen looked up to heaven and said he saw Jesus standing at the right hand of God, they cast him out of the city and stoned him to death. His last words were a prayer of forgiveness for his murderers.

Right *The painting of* The Apostles St Paul and St Barnabas at Lystra *by Jacob Jordaens (1593–1678) illustrates the incident related in Acts 14 when the people of Lystra mistook the apostles for gods believing Barnabas to be the chief god Jupiter*

Far right *Stephen was the first of a long line of martyrs who forfeited their lives because of their Christian belief. The* Stoning of St Stephen *is by Adam Elsheimer (c. 1574–1610)*

MIRACLES OF THE BIBLE

There are various words which are translated as "miracles," "wonders," "mighty acts," and so forth in English versions of the Bible. They refer to God's provision for his people in the manifestation of his power, both in "natural" and in apparently "supernatural" events. The miracles discussed here are all miracles in the sense of extraordinary events resulting from divine intervention.

MIRACLES OF THE OLD TESTAMENT

The earliest miracles in the Bible are the miraculous pregnancies of old or barren women (e.g. Gen. 18:11, 21:1–2), a phenomenon that recurs throughout the Bible. However, the first of God's people to experience spectacular miracles was **Moses**.

Moses' first miraculous encounter happened when he was in **Midian** and God spoke to him from the middle of a bush that was on fire but did not burn up (Ex. 3). In order to convince Moses that he would be able to lead the Israelites out of Egypt, God performed two more miracles: he turned Moses' rod into a snake, and made his hand momentarily leprous (Ex. 4:1–7). By the use of their rods, Moses' and his brother **Aaron** brought down the plagues upon Egypt (Ex. 7–10).

Moses used his rod again to make the waters of the Red Sea part to enable the Israelites to pass through, and then to make the water return to drown the pursuing Egyptians (Ex. 14). This was just the first of many such occurrences the Israelites experienced as they wandered for forty years. These included the miraculous provision of water at Marah and Horeb (Ex. 15:23–25; Num. 20:1–11), the manna and quails (Ex. 16), the blossoming of Aaron's rod (Num.

17), and the brass serpent that healed snake bites (Num. 21:6–9). Moses' successor **Joshua** also caused waters to part (Josh. 3), and the sun and moon stood still at his command (Josh. 10:12–13).

Many of the other miracles of the Old Testament are associated with the prophets **Elijah** and **Elisha**. Some of their miracles recall those of Moses, such as Elijah parting the waters of the Jordan (2 Kgs. 2:8) and Elisha purifying bitter water (2 Kgs. 2:19–22). Elisha's feeding of a hundred men with scant provisions (2 Kgs. 4:42–44) anticipates Jesus' feeding of the five thousand. Both prophets performed healing miracles, including raising from the dead

In these details from early Christian sarcophagi, Jesus is shown performing healing miracles

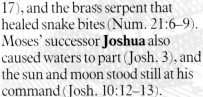

Many of the miracles in the Old Testament were associated with Moses, and one of the most spectacular was the crossing of the Red Sea by the Israelites. This modern picture of the event is by Tamas Galambos

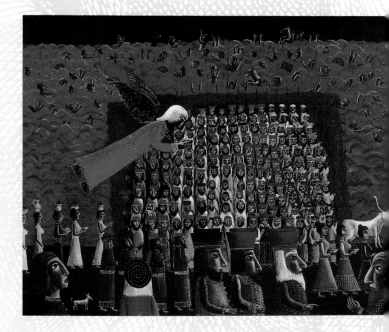

122

One of Jesus' miracles involving mastery over nature is portrayed in The Miraculous Draught of Fishes *by Raphael (1483–1520)*

(1 Kgs. 17:17–24; 2 Kgs. 4:1–37). Elijah's most famous miracle is probably his defeat of the prophets of Baal on Mount Carmel when God sent fire to burn up his sacrifice (1 Kgs. 18:17–38).

Many Old Testament miracles involve the intervention of angels (e.g. **Lot**'s rescue from **Sodom** in Gen. 19:1–22; Balaam's ass in Num. 22:22–35). Others, like Ezekiel being lifted up to the heavens by a lock of his hair (Ezek. 8:1–3), are more in the nature of visions. One other event that comes into neither of these categories is the miracle with the fleece, by which God persuaded **Gideon** that he had been chosen to defeat the Midianites (Judg. 6:36–40).

MIRACLES OF THE NEW TESTAMENT

The story of Jesus begins with his miraculous birth to a virgin and ends with his miraculous resurrection from death.

In his three-year ministry Jesus performed many miracles, the majority of which were concerned with healing of either physical or mental sickness. He restored sight to the blind, speech to the dumb, and hearing to the deaf (e.g. Matt. 9:27–33, 12:22, 20:29–34). He healed people suffering with leprosy, paralysis, and epilepsy (e.g. Matt. 8:2–3, 9:2–7, 17:14–18). He delivered people from demon possession (e.g. Luke 4:33–35, 8:27–35, 11:14). He was able to heal from a distance, without even seeing the sick person (John 4:46–54). On three occasions he raised people from the dead (Luke 7:11–15, 8:41–42, 49–56; John 11:1–44).

Other miracles of Jesus involved a supernatural mastery over natural forces. Many happened on the sea: the calming of the storm (Matt. 8:23–27); Jesus walking on the water (John 6:19–21); two miraculous catches of fish (Luke 5:1–11; John 21:1–11); the coin found in the fish's mouth (Matt. 17:24–27). Other miracles in this category include the feeding of the five thousand (Matt. 14:15–21) and the transformation of water into wine at **Cana** (John 2:1–11). Perhaps Jesus' strangest miracle was his cursing of the unproductive fig tree (Matt. 21:17–20).

After Jesus' death and resurrection, and the coming of the Holy Spirit, the apostles were also empowered to perform miracles. **Peter** and **Paul** healed sickness, cast out demons, and raised the dead (e.g. Acts 3:1–6, 9:36–41, 16:16–18); both were miraculously delivered from prison (Acts 5:17–29, 16:25–33).

PAUL

Meaning of name: Little
Bible reference: Acts 7:58–8: 3, 9:1–30, 13–28; *see also*
Rom., 1 Cor., 2 Cor., Gal., Eph., Phil., Col., 1 Thess.,
2 Thess., 1 Tim., 2 Tim., Titus, Philem.

Apostle and missionary. Originally called Saul, Paul
was a zealous Pharisee and persecutor of the early
Christians, witnessing and approving **Stephen**'s murder. He was converted by a dramatic vision of Jesus
when he was on the road to **Damascus**, and became
one of the leaders of the Church. Paul spent the rest
of his life in extensive and tireless missionary work,
preaching the gospel and establishing churches wher-
ever he went. He was arrested, beaten, and imprisoned
many times, and his life was often in danger.

Paul was a tentmaker by trade, but an educated
man who was an eloquent preacher and clear writer.
His main theological contribution to Christianity is his
exposition of justification by faith.

SIMON THE MAGICIAN

Meaning of name: Hearing
Bible reference: Acts 8:9–24

A magician of **Samaria**. Simon was considered to be
a man with power from God because of his sorcery
but, when **Philip** preached the gospel in Samaria, he
was among the many who believed and were baptized.
Peter and **John** arrived in Samaria and began to lay
hands on the new believers and pray for them to receive
the Holy Spirit. When Simon saw the effect of the
laying-on of hands he longed to have the same power as
the apostles, and offered them money to give him the
power. Peter rebuked him for thinking that spiritual
gifts could be purchased with money.

DORCAS

Meaning of name: Gazelle
Bible reference: Acts 9:36–42

A disciple living at **Joppa**. Dorcas was a charitable
woman who helped the poor and made clothes for
them. When she died her friends were deeply grieved
and sent for **Peter**, who was in nearby Lydda. Peter
arrived and prayed, then told Dorcas to get up. Dorcas
sat up, and Peter called all the believers to witness that
she was alive.

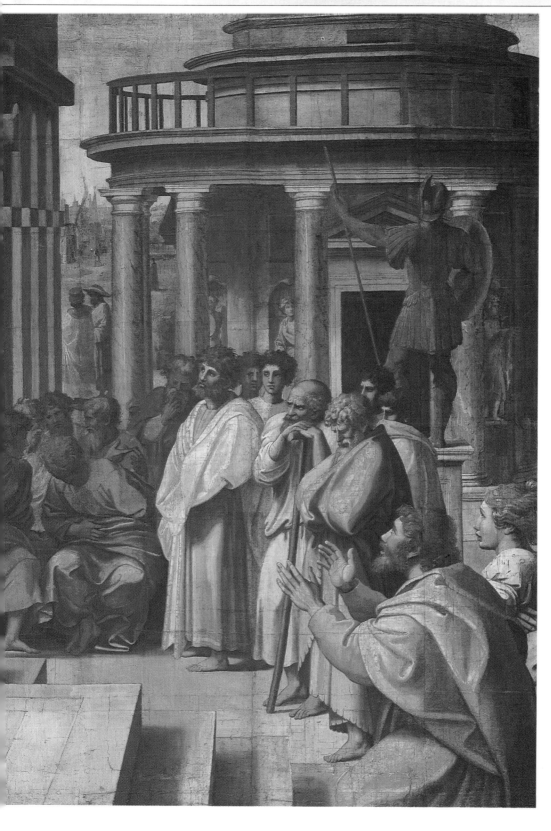

The New Testament letters of Paul form the foundation for the development of Christian theology. The book of Acts shows him as a man of action, overcoming countless obstacles to his missionary vocation, but his primary gift was as a preacher. St Paul Preaching at Athens by Raphael (1483–1520) shows the apostle addressing the people of Athens at the Areopagus, when he condemned their superstition and told them about the real God (Acts 17:16–31)

CORNELIUS

Meaning of name: Horn
Bible reference: Acts 10

A Roman centurion. He is described as a "devout" man, pious and charitable. One day he had a vision of an angel who told him to call for **Peter**, who would tell him what to do. Cornelius sent two of his servants to fetch Peter, who meanwhile had had a vision in which God told him that nothing was unclean that God had made clean. Peter went to Cornelius's house, although Cornelius was a Gentile and normally Jews did not mix with Gentiles. There, he realized that his vision had meant that Gentiles were no longer to be excluded, so he preached the gospel of Jesus to Cornelius. Cornelius and his household believed and received the Holy Spirit. When Peter heard them praising God and speaking in tongues he knew that they should be treated as Christian believers, and baptized them accordingly.

HEROD AGRIPPA I

Meaning of name: Son of the hero
Bible reference: Acts 12:1–6, 19–21

Grandson of Herod the Great. A persecutor of the early Church, he had **James** killed and **Peter** imprisoned.

MARK

Meaning of name: Roman surname associated with the god Mars
Bible reference: Acts 12:12, 25, 13:5, 13, 15:37–39; Col. 4:10; 2 Tim. 4:11; Philem. 24

Companion of **Paul**. Mark's mother was a wealthy Christian widow living in **Jerusalem**, and she was related to **Barnabas**. Mark accompanied Paul and Barnabas to **Cyprus** but left them at Perga. Because of this, when Barnabas wished to take him on their next journey Paul opposed the idea. Unable to agree, they parted, Barnabas going to Cyprus with Mark. The rift with Paul was apparently later healed, for Mark accompanied both him and **Timothy** on subsequent missions.

TIMOTHY

Meaning of name: Honored of God
Bible reference: Acts 16:1–3, 17:14–16, 18:5, 19:22, 20:4; 1 Cor. 4:17, 16:10–11; 2 Cor. 1: 1, 19; Phil. 2:19–23; 1 Thess. 3:2–6; Heb. 13:23; *see also* 1 Tim.; 2 Tim.

Companion of **Paul**. Timothy was the son of a Jewish mother and a Greek father, but was brought up to worship God. He was probably converted to Christianity when Paul visited **Lystra** on his first missionary journey. Timothy accompanied Paul on many of his missions, and the apostle regarded him as a spiritual son.

LYDIA

Meaning of name: The Lydian woman
Bible reference: Acts 16:13–15, 40

A woman from Thyatira. Lydia was a successful businesswoman who dealt in purple dye. She was apparently a Gentile convert to Judaism and was one of a group of women who met by the river at Philippi to pray. When she heard the gospel from **Paul**, Lydia believed and was baptized. She offered hospitality to Paul and his companions, and when Paul and Silas came out of prison they went to Lydia's house.

AQUILA

Meaning of name: Eagle
Bible reference: Acts 18:2–3, 18–19, 26; Rom. 16:3–5

See **Priscilla**.

PRISCILLA

Meaning of name: Ancient, former
Bible reference: Acts 18:2–3, 18–19, 26; Rom. 16:3–5

Fellow-worker with **Paul**. She and her husband **Aquila** were tentmakers by trade, like Paul, and had a close relationship with him. They accompanied him to Syria and **Ephesus**, where he left them, and it was there that they met **Apollos** and made themselves responsible for instructing him in the Christian faith (*see* **Apollos**).

APOLLOS

Meaning of name: From Apollonia
Bible reference: Acts 18:24–19:1; 1 Cor. 1:12, 3:4–6, 22, 4:6, 16:12

An Alexandrian Jew. He appeared in Ephesus in AD 52, and preached eloquently in the synagogues. He knew about Jesus, but his knowledge was incomplete. However, instructed by **Priscilla** and **Aquila**, he went on to become a reliable and successful preacher. His influence became such that factions arose of those loyal to his preaching as opposed to **Paul**'s, but it is clear that neither man desired such party followings, and Paul regarded Apollos as a fellow-worker for the gospel.

HEROD AGRIPPA II

Meaning of name: Son of the hero
Bible reference: Acts 25:13–26:2, 26:27–32

Son of **Herod Agrippa I**. When imprisoned by the governor Festus, **Paul** appealed to Herod Agrippa and defended himself before him. The king declared that he could not see that Paul deserved any punishment.

LUKE

Meaning of name: From Lucania
Bible reference: Col. 4:14; 2 Tim. 4:11; Philem. 24

Fellow-worker with **Paul**. Luke is described as a physician, and a close companion of Paul. He was the author of the third Gospel, the most literary of the Gospels, and the book of Acts, some of which is written in the first person.

Far left *In this picture of St Mark, from the ninth-century Ebbo Gospels, the evangelist is shown in the composition of his Gospel*

Above *The representation of the evangelist St Luke comes from an eleventh-century version of the Gospels in Latin, compiled by German monks*

There are no songs comparable to the songs of Zion, no orations equal to those of the prophets, and no politics like those which the Scriptures teach.
JOHN MILTON 1608–1674

ANIMALS AND BIRDS IN THE BIBLE

The Bible abounds with references to all kinds of animals. The animals discussed here are a selection of the many that are named in both Old and New Testaments. It should be noted that in earlier versions of the Bible, translations of animal names are often inaccurate. Little was known about the Palestinian wildlife of Bible times until about the nineteenth century, and earlier translators tended to use the names of familiar European animals.

This scene from the Vienna Genesis probably represents Rebekah giving refreshment to Abraham's servant and his camels (Gen. 24)

MAMMALS

Sheep

Mentioned over four hundred times, in a dozen different Hebrew words and four Greek ones sheep are perhaps the most important animals in the Bible. They were domesticated for their wool and for meat, though in fact the meat was normally eaten only at sacrificial meals. Sheep milk was a more important food source, usually consumed in the form of curds. Sheepskins were used for clothing, and rams' horns as musical instruments (Josh. 6:4) and oil containers (1 Sam. 16:1).

Sheep are more often used in spiritual metaphors. The one-time shepherd **David** wrote that the Lord was his shepherd, and Jesus is referred to both as the Good Shepherd and the Lamb of God.

Cattle

The word "cattle" is often used very generally to denote all domesticated livestock. Domesticated cattle were descended from the wild ox, which is sometimes translated "unicorn" (e.g. Deut. 33:17). Cattle were first kept for milk; later the bulls were used in agriculture for drawing loads and as beasts of burden. Cows were used to carry the Ark of the Covenant back to Israel (1 Sam. 6).

Goats

Goats were usually herded along with sheep, which explains the reference to "separating the sheep from the goats" (Matt. 26:32). They were valued for their ability to thrive on rougher land. They were used for their milk and skins as well as for food. The story of **Jacob** obtaining the blessing intended for **Esau** involved a goat-meat stew (Gen. 27).

Camels

Camels are, of course, peculiarly adapted to life in dry regions, so they were highly valued. They are mentioned as part of the wealth of **Abraham** and **Jacob** (Gen. 12:16, 30:43). They were used for transport and as beasts of burden,

Goats were valued in Bible times for they could live happily on rough and unfertile land. They are still reared in the same areas today

and their hair was woven into cloth (Matt. 3:4). The camel counted as an unclean animal, so it was not used for food.

Asses
Two Hebrew words are translated as "ass" (or "donkey" in more modern versions) and refer to the domesticated ass. Of the two words generally translated as "wild ass," one of them would be better rendered as "onager." Asses were used mainly for transport and as beasts of burden. The only talking animal in the Bible, apart from the serpent of Genesis 3, was Balaam's ass (Num. 22). Jesus rode into Jerusalem on an ass (Matt. 21:1–9), as prophesied in Zechariah 9:9.

Horses
Horses were used not so much as transport or as beasts of burden, but as cavalry. They are frequently mentioned as symbols of war and

Horses were kept only by the rich and powerful, and usually used in war. This picture from an Assyrian relief shows a horse drawing a chariot. It dates from the reign of Ashurbanipal, about 650 BC

power (e.g. 2 Kgs. 6:17; Rev. 6:2–8). The Egyptians rode horses to pursue the Israelites in Exodus 14. **David**'s sons **Absalom** and **Solomon** both kept horses and chariots (2 Sam. 15:1; 1 Kgs. 10:26–29).

Asses appear both at the beginning and end of Jesus' life. Before the Crucifixion, he rode into Jerusalem on an ass, and as a baby he was taken to Egypt on an ass (or so tradition holds – the Scriptures do not actually mention an ass). This illustration of The Flight into Egypt *comes from the Hastings Book of Hours (c. 1480)*

Pigs
Pigs were unclean animals and were not domesticated by the Israelites. The Old Testament mentions wild boar (e.g. Ps. 80:13). In Jesus' time pigs were kept by Gentiles, and New Testament references to them are always tinged with distaste. Demons cast out by Jesus entered into a herd of pigs (Mark 5:1–13). Jesus warns against casting pearls before swine (Matt. 7:6), and the Prodigal Son in the parable is reduced to utter degradation when he has to tend pigs (Luke 15).

Dogs
Although dogs were domesticated in other parts of the world, and were used for hunting in Egypt, they were regarded with loathing by the Israelites, who knew them only as unclean scavengers. The horror of **Jezebel**'s death was intensified by her body being eaten by dogs (2 Kgs. 9:36), and the

word "dog" is used in the New Testament metaphorically for various kinds of undesirable people (e.g. Phil. 3:2; Rev. 22:15).

Lions
Lions were quite common in Old Testament Palestine, although they disappeared from the area about six hundred years ago. There are nine different Hebrew words used for "lion." They were associated with royalty and often kept in captivity in royal palaces, as in the story of **Daniel** (Dan. 6). Lions were killed by **David** (1 Sam. 17:35), **Samson** (Judg. 14:6), and David's soldier Benaiah (2 Sam. 23:20). They often occur in visions (e.g. Ezek. 1:10; Dan. 7:4).

Lions were kept for sport by the kings of Mesopotamia. This relief from the palace of the Assyrian king Ashurbanipal shows a lion released from its cage for a hunt

Bears
The bear mentioned in the Bible would be the Syrian brown bear, which is still found in some parts of the Middle East. It appears to have been feared more than the lion (Amos 5:19). Bears occur in a curious story in 2 Kings 2:23–24, where little children who mocked **Elisha** because of his baldness are eaten by bears.

The snake has always been abhorred because of its role in the story of the fall. This picture of Adam and Eve and the serpent comes from a sixteenth-century Limoges plaque

REPTILES AND INSECTS

Snakes

The word "serpent" is sometimes used to mean a snake and sometimes applied to creeping reptiles in general. Several different Hebrew words are used, variously translated as "asp," "adder," and "viper." The asp was probably a cobra. There were several species of adder and viper, including the desert viper, which is sometimes translated as "cockatrice." The fear with which snakes were regarded is exemplified by the identification of Satan as a serpent in Genesis 3. The brass serpent used by **Moses** (Num. 21:6–9) to cure the bite of "fiery serpents" (probably carpet vipers) was later used as an object of worship (2 Kgs. 18:4). Most New Testament references are metaphorical (e.g. Jesus refers to the Pharisees as vipers in Matt. 23:33), but **Paul** was bitten by a viper in Acts 28:3–6.

Lizards

Lizards were, and still are, the most common reptile found in Israel and surrounding countries. There were many different species and some of the animal names given by inaccurate translators probably really referred to lizards. In the list of unclean "creeping things" in Leviticus 11:29–30, the "ferret" is probably a gecko, the "tortoise" a spiny-tailed lizard, the "snail" a skink, and the "mole" perhaps a kind of chameleon.

Locusts

Locusts are the insects most often mentioned in the Bible, with nine different Hebrew names. They are thought of primarily as destroyers of crops, and there are several references to plagues of locusts (e.g. Ex. 10:13–15; Joel 1:4). Locusts were, however, permitted as food (Lev. 11:22) and were eaten by **John the Baptist** in the wilderness (Mark 1:6).

Other Insects

Ants, bees, and wasps were all common. The ant is commended for its industry in Proverbs 6:6–8 and 30:25. Most references to bees are to the honey bee (e.g. Judg. 14:8), which was obviously much prized. The only wasp mentioned is the large, fierce hornet (e.g. Ex. 23:28). Flies and fleas were common nuisances and could also carry disease. Gnats (sometimes translated as "lice") and flies were among the plagues in Exodus 8. The only reference to butterflies or moths in the Bible is to the clothes moth (Job 4:19; Luke 12:33).

The desert locust. Locusts have always been dreaded for their ability to destroy huge areas of crops in a very short time

BIRDS

Birds of Prey

There were many birds of prey in the region, and several are listed as forbidden food in Leviticus 11:13–18. The bird sometimes translated as "gier eagle" is thought to be the Egyptian vulture, the "ossifrage" was the bearded vulture, and the "bald eagle" of Micah 1:16 is probably the griffon vulture. Although eagles did exist, the word often seems to be misapplied to vultures, for example, the "eagles" in Matthew 24:28 which are said to gather round a carcass.

Above *The white dove. The dove has a special significance as a symbol of the Holy Spirit, which descended on Jesus in the form of a dove at his baptism (Luke 3:22)*

I KINGS.
Chap. XVII. V. 6.

Elijah fed by Ravens

Above *The story of the ravens bringing bread and meat to the prophet Elijah is illustrated in this engraving*

Pigeons and Doves

There were several species which are usually translated as "dove" or as "young pigeon." The rock dove was used as food and for message-carrying and this was probably the bird referred to in the account of **Noah** and the flood (Gen. 8:8–11). Turtle doves and pigeons were used often as sacrificial birds (e.g. Lev. 1:14; Num. 6:10; John 2:14). They are mentioned often in the Song of Solomon, where the writer compares his beloved's eyes to the eyes of a dove (4:1) and calls her "my dove" (6:9).

Ravens

Ravens and crows were both common. The raven was the first bird released from the ark (Gen. 8:6–7), and **Elijah** was said to have been fed by ravens when he was in hiding (1 Kgs. 17:6).

Sparrows

The "sparrows" that Jesus mentions as being sold at two for a farthing (Matt. 10:29) could be any of various small birds that were hunted and sold at that time. Sparrows also occur in Psalms 84 (v.3) and 102 (v.7), although the latter reference is thought to be more applicable to the blue rock thrush than to the house sparrow.

Domestic Fowl

These are not mentioned at all in the Old Testament, although fowls were domesticated in ancient times. Jesus uses the hen figuratively when talking of his love for Jerusalem (Matt. 23:37). The cock, or rooster, is mentioned in its role as morning alarm in Mark 13:35 and, of course, in the story of **Peter**'s betrayal of Jesus.

The Dome of the Rock, Jerusalem

BIBLE PLACES

The geographical area covered by the Bible takes in not just the traditional "Bible lands," but stretches over three continents. Some of the places mentioned in the Bible are still thriving; others have been uninhabited for centuries. The most significant places are discussed in the following section.

BIBLE PLACES

Judaea and Canaan

BETHANY

A village just outside **Jerusalem**, by the eastern slope of the Mount of Olives on the **Jericho** road. It remains today, with an Arab population of around seven hundred, although its modern name is El-Azariyah. This name is a reference to **Lazarus**, for Bethany was the village where Jesus' friend lived, with his sisters **Martha** and **Mary**. It was here that Jesus was anointed (Matt. 26:6–13; Mark 14:3–9); here (though the name of the village is not mentioned) that Jesus was served by Martha and commended Mary for listening to his teaching; here that Lazarus was raised from the dead (John 11). The Bethany on the River Jordan (sometimes rendered "Bethabara") where John the Baptist was operating (John 1:28) has not been identified by scholars.

BETHEL

A small settlement about twelve miles north of **Jerusalem**, on the watershed route. Archeological excavations suggest that there was a prosperous city here in the Middle Bronze Age, which was destroyed in about 1550 BC and replaced by a later settlement, which was also destroyed and rebuilt. At an early stage it became an Israelite settlement, and it flourished in the early days of the monarchy. The city was rebuilt as a Roman township in the first century AD. It is now an Arab village called Tell Beitin.

Bethel is first mentioned as a place where **Abraham** pitched his tent and built an altar (Gen. 12:8). **Jacob** had his vision of the ladder (Gen. 28:10–22) there, and is said to have renamed the place Bethel (house of God) from its original name, Luz. It was looked on as a holy place when the ark was kept there, but under Rehoboam it became a center of idolatrous worship (1 Kgs. 12–13).

BETHLEHEM

A town five miles south of **Jerusalem**. It was a Philistine garrison town, and was later fortified by Rehoboam. Once famed as the city of **David**, it had become an obscure village at the time of Jesus' birth. It was desecrated by the Roman emperor Hadrian in the second century AD, but the Church of the Nativity was built by Constantine two centuries later. The town now has the Arab name Bayt Lahm, with the same meaning: house of bread.

Bethlehem is first mentioned as being close to **Rachel**'s burial place (Gen. 35:19), when it was called

The River Jordan, an important source of water for the Holy Land, is fed by streams such as the Hazbani (**top left**) and the Banyas (**bottom left**). Banyas is a corruption of the name of the god Pan to whom the Syrian-Greeks dedicated the stream

Above The Mount of Olives, seen through one of the arches on Jerusalem's Temple Mount. It was from here that Jesus rode into Jerusalem in triumph

There are 3,566,480 letters in the Bible, and between 773,692 and 773,746 words, varying according to how hyphenation is counted.

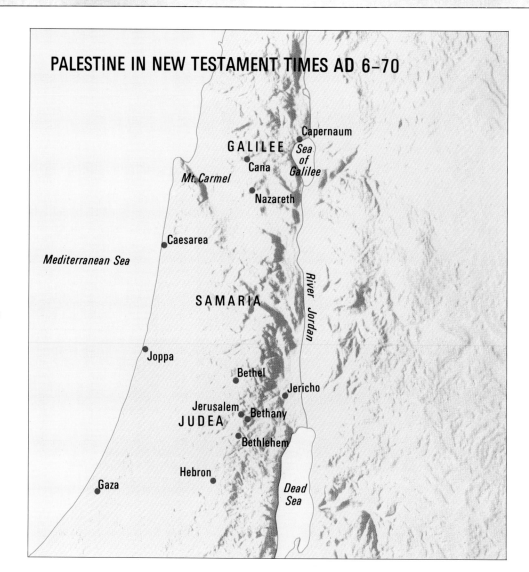

PALESTINE IN NEW TESTAMENT TIMES AD 6–70

Right Judea and Galilee in the time of Christ

Far right The Church of the Holy Sepulchre in Jerusalem, believed to be Golgotha, site of the Crucifixion and burial of Christ. Although now within the city walls, it was outside them in Christ's time

Ephrath. It was the home of **Boaz**, who married **Ruth**, and their descendant Jesse, David's father, continued to live there (1 Sam. 16). It was prophesied that the Messiah would be born in Bethlehem (Mic. 5:2); when Jesus was born, **Herod**'s priests reminded him of this prophecy, and the wise men were sent to look for the child in Bethlehem (Matt. 2:1–8).

CAESAREA

Caesarea was built by **Herod the Great** between 22 and 10 BC and became the Roman metropolis of **Judaea** and official residence of the Roman procurators. It was

a seaport, situated about twenty-three miles south of **Mount Carmel**, and a busy maritime and commercial center with a mixed population. The city was destroyed in the thirteenth century.

Caesarea was the scene of the conversion of **Cornelius** (Acts 10), and the home of **Philip** and his prophetess daughters (Acts 21:8–16). **Paul** was sent to Caesarea by the governor Felix, was imprisoned for two years, and subsequently testified to **Agrippa** and Festus (Acts 23:23–33; chaps 25–26).

CALVARY

Site of the Crucifixion, outside the city walls of **Jerusalem**. The name Calvary is a translation of Golgotha, which means "skull," and was so named either because it was a place of execution or because it was shaped like a skull. The site has not been exactly identified. Both the present Garden Tomb and the Church of the Holy Sepulcher are claimed to be the site of Calvary, but though the latter is more likely, scholars are still doubtful about its claims.

The name Calvary is used only in the Gospel of Luke (Luke 23:33). In the account of the Crucifixion in the other Gospels the name Golgotha is used (e.g. Matt. 27:33).

CANAAN

It is difficult to give an exact location for Canaan, as the name is not always applied in the same way. The original land of Canaan appears to have been the Phoenician coastal area, including the **Jordan** valley. The designation is also applied to a wider area, cover-

> *When you read God's word, you must constantly be saying to yourself, it is talking to me, and about me.*
> SØREN KIERKEGAARD 1813–1855

ing all of what came to be called Palestine. The first Semitic settlers were already in the area before 3000 BC and Canaanite cities were established by 2000 BC. After a period of Egyptian domination, Canaan was conquered by the Israelites at the end of the thirteenth century BC, and the former Canaanites became concentrated in the area of Tyre and Sidon.

Canaan has great significance in the Old Testament as the Promised Land, the land "flowing with milk and honey" that God promised to the Hebrew people. **Moses** sent spies to search out the land (Num. 12–13), and the conquest and settlement of Canaan is described in the book of Joshua.

The Supper at Emmaus *by Caravaggio (1573–1610) shows the moment when the resurrected Jesus, dining at the house of disciples at Emmaus, broke bread and was at last recognized by his hosts*

EMMAUS

A village a few miles from **Jerusalem**. It has not been possible to identify this village, although many attempts have been made.

Two disciples, Cleopas and another, were walking to Emmaus after the Crucifixion, and discussing the events, when they were joined by the resurrected Jesus, whom they failed to recognize. He talked to them and when they reached Emmaus they offered him hospitality. When Jesus blessed the bread they knew him at last, but he vanished (Luke 24:13–35).

GETHSEMANE

A garden near the Mount of Olives, east of **Jerusalem** beyond the Kidron valley. The exact site is disputed, and two adjacent sites are claimed to be the original garden.

Jesus and his disciples went to Gethsemane the night before he was crucified, and Jesus prayed in the garden while the disciples slept. **Judas** brought the soldiers there and Jesus was arrested (Matt. 26:36–56).

GOLGOTHA

See **Calvary**

HEBRON

A city in the mountains twenty miles south-west of **Jerusalem**. It is thought to have been built about 1750 BC although its biblical associations go back even earlier. The city survived various occupations but was burned by the Romans in the first century AD. It was revived by the Muslims and is now a thriving town in Jordan.

Abraham lived in Hebron (Gen. 13:18) and he, **Sarah**, **Isaac**, **Rebekah**, **Jacob**, and **Leah** were all buried there. **Joshua** gave Hebron to Caleb (Josh. 14:13–14). **David** lived there for several years and was anointed king of Judah and Israel there (2 Sam. 2:1–4, 5:1–3), and it was the center of his son **Absalom**'s revolt (2 Sam. 15).

JERICHO

An ancient city six miles west of the River Jordan, and ten miles north of the Dead Sea. It was a fertile region and was probably inhabited from 8000 BC. It declined but was revived as a walled city in the Early Bronze Age. At the time of the Old Testament patriarchs it had again been sacked and resettled. After **Joshua**'s destruction of Jericho in the thirteenth century BC, the city lay in ruins for centuries, although the site was still sporadically inhabited. The New Testament town was

situated south of the original city. The city has changed its site several times since, and the modern Jericho in Jordan is on the site of the city built by the Crusaders.

When Joshua conquered Jericho he laid a curse on anyone who rebuilt the city (Josh. 6:26), which was fulfilled when Hiel the Bethelite attempted the rebuilding (1 Kgs. 16:34). **Elijah** and **Elisha** lived at Jericho at one time (2 Kgs. 2:4–5). Jericho figures in the New Testament stories of the healing of Bartimaeus (Mark 10:46–52) and the conversion of **Zacchaeus** (Luke 19:1–9).

Top left The monastery of Abraham's oak tree at Hebron

Above Remains of the palaces built by Herod the Great and his successors at Jericho have been discovered. The picture shows Hisham's palace

Left Agony in the Garden by Giovanni Bellini (?1430–1516) shows Jesus praying in the garden of Gethsemane before his arrest, while Peter, James and John sleep

JERUSALEM

City set in the hills of **Judah**, west of the Dead Sea. Its history goes back to the Stone Age. It was settled by a Semitic people in about 2500 BC, and when the Israelites entered **Canaan** it was in the hands of the Jebusites. The city was not completely captured by the Israelites until **David**'s time. In 587 BC it was destroyed by the Babylonians, and it remained in ruins until about 445 BC when Nehemiah began the rebuilding of the walls. In 332 BC the city was taken by Alexander the Great, but it subsequently suffered much damage under Egyptian and Syrian occupation. The Jews, under Judas Maccabaeus, recaptured Jerusalem in 165 BC, but it fell to Rome about a hundred years later. **Herod the Great** rebuilt the temple in 37 BC, but it was destroyed again under Titus in AD 70. The city was under the domination of various foreign powers until 1967. The present city walls were built by the Turks in 1542.

Jerusalem is of great significance in both Old and New Testaments. Probably the most important Old Testament events to take place there were David's conquest of the city (2 Sam. 5:6–10), **Solomon**'s building of the temple there (1 Kgs. 5–8), the fall of Jerusalem and destruction of the temple (2 Kgs. 24–25), and Ezra's and Nehemiah's restoration. Jesus was dedicated in the temple at Jerusalem as a baby, and conversed with the teachers there as a twelve-year-old (Luke 2:22–49). He entered Jerusalem riding a donkey and cast out the money changers from the temple (Mark 11:1–19); and his trial, crucifixion, and resurrection all happened in or just outside the city. The first seven chapters of Acts describe the growth of the early Church at Jerusalem.

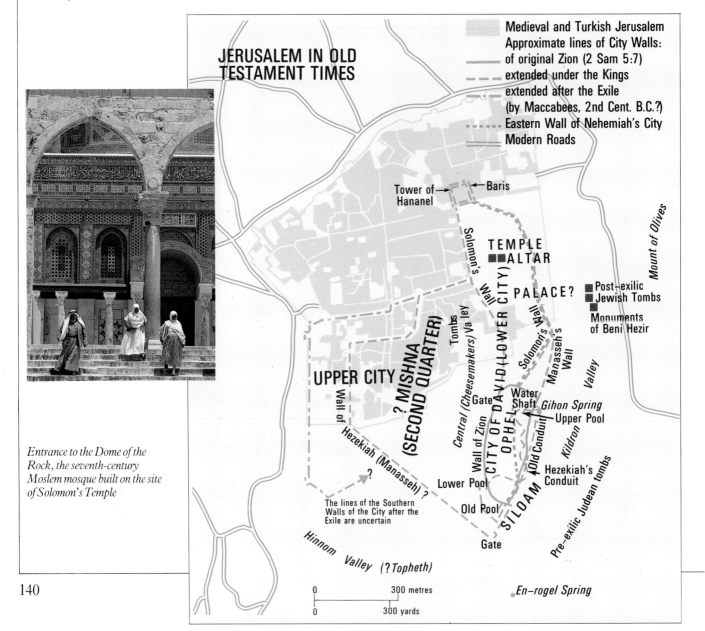

Entrance to the Dome of the Rock, the seventh-century Moslem mosque built on the site of Solomon's Temple

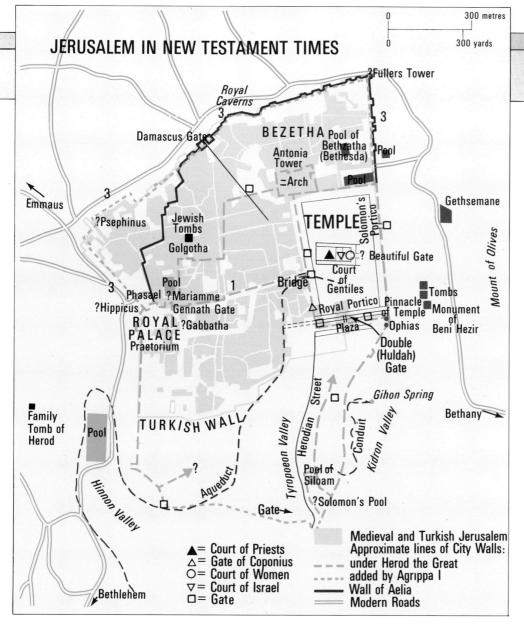

JERUSALEM IN NEW TESTAMENT TIMES

0   300 metres
0   300 yards

?Fullers Tower

Royal Caverns

3

Damascus Gate

BEZETHA

Pool of Bethzatha (Bethesda)

Antonia Tower

Pool

3

= Arch

Pool

Emmaus

3

Gethsemane

?Psephinus

Jewish Tombs

Golgotha

TEMPLE

Solomon's Portico

Mount of Olives

? Beautiful Gate

Court of Gentiles

Bridge

3

Pool

Phasael   ?Mariamme

1

?Hippicus   Gennath Gate

ROYAL PALACE   ?Gabbatha

Praetorium

Royal Portico

Tombs

Pinnacle of Temple

Monument of Beni Hezir

Plaza   Ophias

Double (Huldah) Gate

Family Tomb of Herod

Pool

TURKISH WALL

Herodian Street

Tyropoeon Valley

Gihon Spring

Bethany

Conduit

Kidron Valley

?

Aqueduct

Pool of Siloam

Hinnon Valley

Gate

?Solomon's Pool

Bethlehem

▲ = Court of Priests
△ = Gate of Coponius
○ = Court of Women
▽ = Court of Israel
□ = Gate

Medieval and Turkish Jerusalem
Approximate lines of City Walls:
- - - under Herod the Great
······ added by Agrippa I
▬▬▬ Wall of Aelia
═══ Modern Roads

Left Jerusalem in New Testament times

Far left Jerusalem in Old Testament times

Below left The Western Wall in Jerusalem, known as the Wailing Wall, where Jews traditionally pray and lament the loss of the temple

Below An imaginary view of the city of Jerusalem by Didier Barra (Monsu Desiderio)

JOPPA

Ancient city and seaport, founded in the seventeenth century BC or earlier. It was given to the tribe of Dan after the Israelite conquest of **Canaan**, but was conquered by the Philistines, and was under various foreign occupations until the Jews recaptured it in the second century BC. It is now called Jaffa and is just south of Tel Aviv.

Joppa features in the story of **Jonah**, as the port from which the prophet set sail for Tarshish instead of going to **Nineveh** (Jon. 1:3). **Peter** raised **Dorcas** at Joppa (Acts 9:36–43), and it was there he had his vision before the conversion of **Cornelius** (Acts 10).

JUDEA

Judea is the name of various Roman administrative regions, more or less corresponding to Judah, the southern kingdom after the division. It stretches from the Philistine plain to the Dead Sea. The split from Israel occurred in 931 BC, when the first separate monarchy of Judah under Rehoboam was established. The kingdom continued until 587 BC, when Judah fell to the Babylonians. After the exile, the political significance of Judah was lost, but the name remains in the words Judaism and Jew. The Roman region of Judea is sometimes used in the New Testament to denote the whole of the Western Palestine area.

The reigns of the kings of Judah are described in the books of Kings and Chronicles. Judea is referred to

*The ancient city and seaport of Joppa is now Jaffa, part of the conurbation of Tel Aviv, and famous for its orange-growing. The photo of Jaffa **above** shows the old city, while the picture on the **right**, dated 1887, represents Joppa seen from the south-west*

throughout the New Testament as: the birthplace of Jesus (**Bethlehem** in Judea); the area where **John the Baptist** preached (the wilderness of Judea – i.e. the desert to the west of the Dead Sea); and the Roman administrative region in general.

SILOAM

A cistern or reservoir fed by the spring of Gihon, on the outskirts of **Jerusalem**. The tunnel connecting the pool to the spring was built by Hezekiah when threatened with Assyrian invasion in around 700 BC (2 Chron. 32:30). The Old Pool was still in use in New Testament times, and remains of a bath-house of the period have been found on the site.

Jesus healed a man blind from birth by putting clay on his eyes and sending him to wash in the Pool of Siloam. This led to a dispute with the Pharisees because the healing took place on the Sabbath (John 9). The tower of Siloam, which fell, killing eighteen people, is referred to by Jesus (Luke 13:4) and is thought to have been sited above the pool.

SODOM

One of the five "cities of the plain" in the Dead Sea region. The cities were destroyed by "fire and brimstone" – probably some kind of seismic event – and their exact location has never been established.

Sodom is first mentioned as the place **Lot** chose as a home (Gen. 13:10–13). In Genesis 14 Lot was captured when Sodom was involved in war. Genesis 19 describes how Lot entertained angels in his house and was besieged by men of Sodom, wanting sex with his visitors. Lot and his family fled from Sodom just in time to escape its destruction but Lot's wife looked back at the city and was turned into a pillar of salt. Sodom became synonymous with sin throughout the Bible. Ezekiel 16:49–51 lists the sins of Sodom as pride, haughtiness and neglect of the poor and needy.

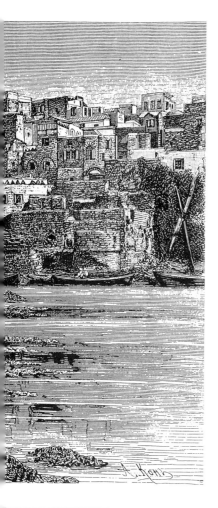

*The Judean desert, shown **above**, is the same area as the wilderness of Judea where John the Baptist preached*

Galilee and Samaria

The Sea of Galilee is actually a very large lake

CANA

A village in the highlands west of the sea of **Galilee**. There are two places with claims to be on the site of the original Cana: Kefr Kenna, a village about four miles north-east of **Nazareth** on the road to Tiberias, and Khirbet Kana, a ruined site some nine miles north of Nazareth.

Cana is mentioned only in John's Gospel. It was the place where Jesus performed his first miracle, turning water into wine at the wedding feast (2:1–11), and also the scene of a later miracle when Jesus healed the son of a nobleman, without even seeing the child (4:46–54). It is also mentioned as the home town of **Nathanael** (21:2).

CAPERNAUM

A town on the north-west shore of the sea of **Galilee**. It was a garrison town, an administrative center, and a customs post. Capernaum is thought to have been inhabited from the first century BC until the seventh century AD. Although there was a rival site at Khirbet Minyeh, modern scholars are now convinced that the city was at Tell Hum, where remains of the synagogue and other evidence of a Jewish settlement have been found.

Capernaum was Jesus' second home (Matt. 4:13; John 2:12) and it was from here that he called **Peter**, **Andrew**, and **Matthew**. It was here, too, that Jesus met the centurion whose servant he healed (Matt. 8:5–13), and he also preached in the synagogue (Mark 1:21). Jesus walked on the water near Capernaum, and when he was back on the shore he preached of himself as the bread of life (John 6). Jesus condemned the inhabitants of Capernaum for their disbelief, despite all the miracles he had performed there (Matt. 11:23–24).

CARMEL

A mountain range about fifteen miles long running north-west to south-east over an area south of the modern Israeli town of Haifa. Mount Carmel is the main ridge. It was sacred to both Baal and Yahweh, and in the sixth century BC was sacred to Jupiter. There are records of a monastery there from AD 570, and subsequent monasteries on the site have been built and destroyed. Mount Carmel was the scene for the dramatic contest between **Elijah** and the prophets of Baal (1 Kgs. 18:18–46).

The town of Carmel in Judah, where Nabal and **Abigail** lived (1 Sam. 25), is a few miles south-east of **Hebron,** and is now called Khirbet el-Karmil.

GALILEE

A region in northern Israel. Its boundaries are not precise, but as a Roman province it was an area bounded on the east by the River Jordan and the Sea of Galilee, and separated from the Mediterranean coast by Syrophoenicia. The fertile area was Lower Galilee. The Sea of Galilee, is a lake in the region, fourteen miles long, through which the Jordan flows. Being cut off from the rest of Israel by Gentile nations, the Galileans were traditionally regarded as provincial and uncouth by southern Jews. Little is known of the region's history before New Testament times, when it was under Roman domination.

Galilee is the scene for many of the Gospel narratives, as it was where Jesus lived and where most of his ministry was carried out. Isaiah prophesied that the Messiah would come from Galilee (Is. 9:1–2) and Jesus' preaching confirmed the prophecy (Matt. 4:12–17). The disciples **Peter**, **Andrew**, **James**, and **John** were

The New Testament is the very best book that ever was or ever will be known in the world.
CHARLES DICKENS 1812–1870

The village of Cana has become famous as the scene of Jesus' first miracle, when he turned water into wine when the drink ran out at a wedding celebration. This picture of The Marriage Feast at Cana *is by Juan de Flandres (1496–c. 1519)*

Left A view across the Dead Sea, with Jordan in the distance

Below right The Jordan valley has changed little since Biblical times

called from their nets on the Sea of Galilee; it was on this lake that Jesus calmed the storm (Matt. 8:23–27) and walked on the water (Matt. 14:22–32); and on its shores that Jesus fed the five thousand (Matt. 14:15–21).

JORDAN

River flowing from Mount Hermon, through the Sea of **Galilee**, to the Dead Sea. The valley was inhabited from about 5000 BC, and city states began to emerge from the end of the fourth millennium BC, though many were destroyed in nomadic invasions. The most settled areas were around Galilee; the Dead Sea area was and is arid and infertile.

The Jordan valley was the territory chosen by **Lot**, when he and **Abraham** parted (Gen. 13). The Israelites' crossing of the river is described in Joshua 3–4. It was on the banks of the Jordan that **Elijah** was taken up to heaven (2 Kgs. 2:1–15), and **Elisha** healed Naaman of leprosy by making him bathe in the Jordan (2 Kgs. 5). **John the Baptist**'s ministry was centered on the Jordan, and Jesus was baptized in the river (Luke 3:1–22).

NAZARETH

Town in the hills of southern Lebanon, midway between the Sea of **Galilee** and the Mediterranean. Nothing is known of Nazareth before New Testament times, when it was under Roman rule. The present Israeli town is probably a little to the west of the original

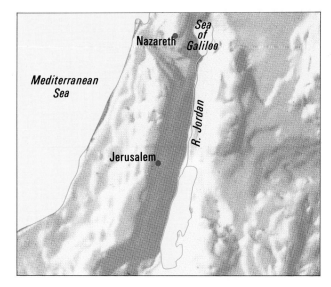

> *What you bring away from the Bible depends to some extent on what you carry to it.*
> OLIVER WENDELL HOLMES 1809–1894

Nazareth.

Mary and **Joseph** returned to Nazareth after their stay in Egypt (Matt. 2:19–23), and all Jesus' early life was spent there. At the start of his ministry Jesus preached in the synagogue at Nazareth, but because they recognized him as a local man of no status, the people refused to accept him (Luke 4:16–30) and he could perform no miracles there (Matt. 13:53–58). Being in an area cut off from the rest of Israel (*see* **Galilee**), Nazareth was despised by many Jews. **Nathanael**, on first hearing of Jesus, asked, "Can any good thing come out of Nazareth?" (John 1:45–46).

SAMARIA

Capital of the northern kingdom of Israel; also a designation used for the surrounding area. It was situated on a hill about six miles north of what is now Nablus in Jordan. There is evidence of habitation from the Early Bronze Age but the city was founded by King Omri in around 880 BC. The construction was continued by **Ahab**, in whose reign the city became a center of idolatrous worship. It was besieged by the Assyrians several times until in 721 BC the king of Assyria deported over 27,000 captives from Samaria, replacing them with colonists from the Assyrian empire. Samaria declined, and was destroyed by Alexander in the fourth century BC, but was rebuilt by Pompey and then **Herod**.

The foundation of the city, its rise, and its fall, are described in the books of Kings (1 Kgs 16–2 Kgs 17). In New Testament times there was deep mutual suspicion and enmity between Jews and the current inhabitants of Samaria. John's account of Jesus' meeting with the Samaritan woman (John 4:1–43) says that Jews have no dealings with Samaritans. It was in Samaria that **Philip**, **Peter**, and **John** encountered **Simon the Magician** (Acts 8:5, 7–24).

The Lands to the South and South-West

EDOM

A mountainous region between the Dead Sea and the Gulf of Aqaba, the traditional home of the descendants of **Esau**. The capital was called Sela, and was near the ancient city of Petra. There is evidence that the Edomites were not the first settlers in the territory, but became the dominant tribe and had established a kingdom before the Israelites did. Edom was conquered first by **Saul**, then by **David**, and was subseqeuntly involved in a series of wars against the Israelites, although at one time it was leagued with Israel against Assyria. Archeological evidence is sparse, but is seems that after being conquered and overrun by Assyrians, Arabs, and Nabateans, Edom had lost its identity by about the third century BC. Many of the inhabitants fled to Judah and were assimilated among the Jews.

Esau was called "Edom" (Gen. 25:30), in memory of the red lentils for which he sold his birthright, because the word is similar to the Hebrew for red. His family had settled in the territory at the time **Jacob** left Laban (Gen. 32:3, 36:8–9). **Moses** sent messengers to the king of Edom asking for passage for the Israelites through their land, but the request was refused (Num. 20:14–21), thereby establishing enmity between the brother nations. Edom suffered massive casualties under **David** and subsequent kings of Israel and Judah (e.g. 1 Kgs. 11:15–16; 2 Kgs. 14:7). Psalm 137 records how Edom rejoiced at the fall of **Jerusalem** (v.7), and many of the prophets foretold Edom's doom because of its hatred (e.g. Ezek. 25:12–14).

EGYPT

Ancient kingdom at the north-east extremity of Africa. The country is mainly desert and today 99 per cent of the inhabitants live in the fertile area near the Nile and its delta which makes up just 4 per cent of the land. There have been settlers in the Nile valley from prehistoric times, but the first pharaoh emerged in about 3000 BC and Egyptian culture began to flourish from that time, reaching a peak in the period from about 2680 to 2180 BC. After this time the power of the kings waned and foreign influences came in, but there were further peaks in Egyptian cultural and political history in 2134–1786 BC and then in 1552–1069 BC. It was during this later period that the Israelite oppression and the Exodus took place. After this there was a long period of decline until Egypt was conquered, first by Alexander the Great in 332 BC, and then by the Romans.

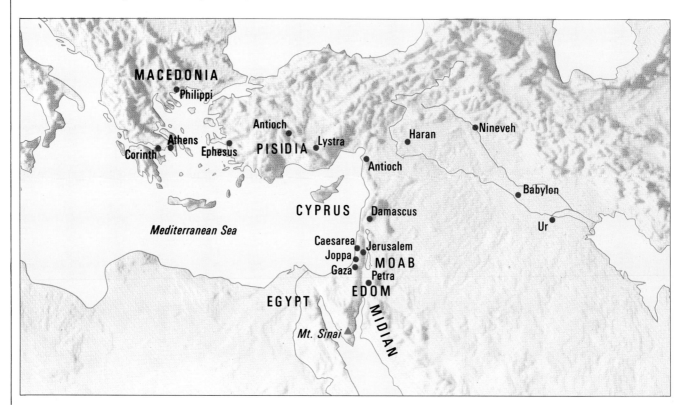

An oasis in the Sinai Desert

The Israelites' association with Egypt began when **Joseph** was sold into slavery there, and eventually flourished and brought his family to live there (Gen. 37–47). The Israelites multiplied in number and were forced into slavery by the Egyptians, who eventually attempted to control their numbers by genocide (Ex. 1). **Moses** escaped the slaughter, was brought up in the royal palace, and finally led the Israelites out of Egypt. When **Herod** sought the life of Jesus, it was to Egypt that **Joseph** and **Mary** fled (Matt. 2:13–14).

GAZA

The most southerly of the five principal Philistine cities. It is situated on the Mediterranean coast near the Israel–Egypt border, and is now part of Egypt. Gaza was used as a military base by Egyptian kings from 1500 BC. It was conquered by **Joshua** but later came under Philistine domination. It changed hands many times over the centuries until captured by Alexander in 332 BC, and it was finally desolated, although a modern city has been built on the site.

Joshua's battles with the city are recorded in Joshua 10:41 and 11:21–22. **Samson** visited a prostitute in Gaza (Judg. 16:1–3) and his death and final revenge on the Philistines took place in Gaza (Judg. 16:21–30).

MIDIAN

A desert region around the gulf of Aqaba, south of **Edom**. The Midianites were descendants of Midian, son of **Abraham** and his concubine Keturah (Gen. 25:1–6). Midian oppressed Israel for seven years until defeated by the army of **Gideon**.

The merchants to whom **Joseph** was originally sold were Midianites (Gen. 37:28–36). **Moses** fled to Midian after killing the Egyptian, and he married there and lived as a shepherd in the region for many years (Ex. 2:15–3:1). Midian later joined **Moab** to conspire against Israel (*see* **Moab**). Gideon's defeat of the Midianites is described in Judges 6–8.

MOAB

A region east of the Jordan and the Dead Sea, north of **Edom**. It was settled by the descendants of Moab, **Lot**'s son by his elder daughter (Gen. 19:37), but was already inhabited before this. Moab became a well-organized kingdom with a distinctive culture. In the time of the judges, Moab oppressed Israel for eighteen years, but it was subdued by **David**. Moab continued to attack Israel but was finally conquered by the Babylonians, then the Persians, and ceased to have an independent existence as a nation.

The king of Moab, Balak, conspired with the Midianites against the Israelites when they were traveling to **Canaan**, by attempting to bribe the prophet Balaam to curse Israel (Num. 22–24). During the Moabite oppression of Israel, **Naomi** and her husband migrated to Moab and their sons married the Moabite women, **Ruth** and Orpah. **Saul**, **David**, and **Solomon** all fought with the Moabites, and after the division, kings of both Israel and Judah continued to battle with Moab.

SINAI

A mountain in the peninsula between the gulfs of Suez and Aqaba (now Sinai Peninsula), also known as Horeb in the Old Testament. Its identity is disputed but both tradition and much modern scholarship points to Jebel Musa ("Mountain of Moses" – about 7,400ft). The surrounding area was known as the wilderness of Sinai (or of Sin).

Mount Sinai's significance is as the place where **Moses** received the law from God (Ex. 19), and all other Bible references to it are within this context.

The Bible is alive, it speaks to me; it has feet, it runs after me; it has hands, it lays hold on me.
MARTIN LUTHER 1483–1546

The Lands to the East

BABYLON

Babylon was the capital city of the area known as Babylonia in south-west Asia, which is now southern Iraq. The city of Babylon stood on the Euphrates river a little north of the modern town of Hillah. Although there is no archeological evidence dating the city from before about 1800 BC, Babel is said to have been founded by Nimrod, **Noah**'s descendant (Gen. 10:9–10), and is thought to have been on the same site as the later Babylon. For many years Babylon struggled for independence under foreign domination, notably Assyrian, until a new Chaldean dynasty was founded in 626 BC and the city was restored. The victorious Babylonian army began to take Jewish captives back to the city, and plundered the temple at **Jerusalem**. Babylon was a religious center where many gods were worshiped – principally Marduk. The city flourished until 539 BC, when the Persians invaded and the king, **Belshazzar**, was killed; eventually it fell into ruins.

The original city of Babel is remembered by the description of the building of the tower, when the people's languages became confused (Gen. 11:1–9). The fall of Jerusalem to the Babylonian king, **Nebuchadnezzar**, is narrated in 2 Kings 24–25, and Babylonian captivity is described in the book of Daniel. The captivity is lamented by many of the prophets, and the destruction of Babylon is foretold (Is. 14:4, 21:9; Jer. 50–51). The Babylon mentioned in Revelations 17–18 is thought to be a symbol for the city of Rome, which was similarly oppressing God's people.

DAMASCUS

The capital city of Syria now and in ancient times. It is situated on the River Barada at the eastern foot of the Anti-Lebanon mountains. Damascus is said to be the oldest continuously inhabited city in the world. It was already a well-established city in 2000 BC. It became a buffer between Assyria and the emergent kingdom of Israel, and figured for centuries in the wars between these states. The city was captured in 734 BC and lost its capital status, which was not restored until 111 BC. From 64 BC to AD 33, Damascus was under the Romans and subsidiary in importance to **Antioch**, but after the Arab conquest of AD 634 it regained its supremacy.

Damascus is first mentioned in Genesis, as the place to which **Abraham** pursued five kings (14:15), and as the home town of Abraham's steward, Eliezer (15:2). **David** captured the city and garrisoned it (2 Sam.

8:5–6), but it became the home of **Solomon**'s adversary, Rezon (1 Kgs. 11:23–25), and grew increasingly powerful under his successors. It was as **Paul** traveled to Damascus that he experienced the vision which brought about his conversion and he was baptized in the city (Acts 9:1–22).

NINEVEH

Ancient capital of the Assyrian empire, situated on the River Tigris, opposite what is now the town of Mosul in north Iraq. The site was occupied from prehistoric

times, but the city is said to have been built by Nimrod, or Asshur (Gen. 10:11). There was a temple dedicated to the goddess Ishtar there in 2300 BC, which was restored in 1800 BC. The city flourished from about 1260 BC until its destruction in 612 BC, when it was attacked by Babylonians and Medes and left in ruins, never to be rebuilt.

The attack of the Assyrian king Sennacherib, and his defeat and return to Nineveh, is described in 2 Kings 18–19. The prophet **Jonah** was sent by God to prophesy against Nineveh, and when he finally did so the people repented and were spared from destruction (Jon. 1:1, 3:1–10). The book of Nahum is a celebration of the fall of Nineveh.

UR

An ancient city, generally identified with a site now occupied by Tell el-Muqayyar on the River Euphrates in southern Iraq. Archeological work on the site indicates occupation from 5000 BC. Remains from graves dating back to 3500 BC have been found, and the ruins of the ancient temple tower still stand. The city was ruled by the Babylonians and Chaldeans, but had ceased to be inhabited by 300 BC.

Ur is mentioned as the home of **Abraham**'s family before they left to travel to **Haran** and then **Canaan** (Gen. 11:28–31, 15:7; Neh. 9:7).

The longest name in the Bible is Maher-shalal-hash-baz (Is. 8:1).

Top *The famous Standard of Ur, which dates from around 2500 BC, is decorated with shell, red limestone and lapis lazuli*

Far left *This glazed-brick relief from the Ishtar gate at Babylon dates from the reign of King Nebuchadnezzar (604-652 BC) and represents a dragon, sacred animal of the god Marduk*

Left *The building of the Tower of Babel, as represented by Pieter Brueghel the Elder (c. 1515–69)*

Greece and Turkey

ANTIOCH

1. Antioch in Syria. Antioch is situated on the River Orontes in what is now south-east Turkey, near the Syrian border. The city was founded in about 300 BC and was the capital of the Roman province of Syria. It became the third largest city of the Roman Empire after it fell to Pompey in 64 BC. It is now called Antalya.

Antioch had a very mixed population of Jews and Gentiles and became a center of early Christianity, second only to **Jerusalem**. During the persecution that followed **Stephen**'s martyrdom, some Christians went to Antioch to preach to the Jews there, and when many Jews and Greeks had been converted, **Barnabas** and **Paul** were sent to Antioch. It was here that the disciples were first given the name "Christians" (Acts 11:19–26). Antioch was at the center of the dispute over whether Gentile converts had to be circumcised (Acts 14:26–15:35; Gal. 2:11).

2. Antioch in Pisidia. This Antioch was a Roman colony situated in an area which is now in central Turkey. The ruins of the city are to be found near the town of Yalvaj. It had been founded by 280 BC and became a free Roman city, Greek-speaking but with a mixed population, including many Jews.

Antioch was a center of civil and military administration at the time that **Paul** visited it on his first missionary journey. Paul preached in the synagogue there, but when he declared that the gospel was also for the Gentiles, some of the Jews roused those in high office in Antioch to organize persecution of Paul and **Barnabas**. They were expelled from the city, but returned later (Acts 13:14–50, 14:19–21).

ATHENS

Athens is the capital of modern Greece and one of the most important cities of antiquity. There appears to have been a city on the site since prehistoric times, but it was in the Classical period of the fourth and fifth

The Bible tells us to love our neighbors, and also to love our enemies; probably because they are generally the same people.
G. K. CHESTERTON 1874–1936

centuries BC that it became renowned as a cultural center. Athens was named for the goddess Athene, but many gods were worshiped there.

The Areopagus (hill of Ares or Mars) no longer exists, but it was once the meeting place for the Athenian tribunal, and it was from here that **Paul** preached his famous sermon (Acts 17:15–34) in which he condemned the superstition and idolatry he saw in Athens, and expounded the true nature of God.

CORINTH

A major trading city on the isthmus between the Greek mainland and the Peloponnese. Corinth began to achieve its importance and prosperity in the sixth and seventh centuries BC. It became part of the Peloponnesian league under Sparta, but later came under Macedonian domination. In the war with the Romans of 146 BC the city was despoiled, but it was rebuilt by Julius Caesar in 46 BC and regained its former prosperity. Corinth was the center of worship of Aphrodite, goddess of love, and was notorious for the immorality of its inhabitants. An earthquake destroyed the old town in 1858 and the subsequent modern town of New Corinth has also been the victim of earthquakes.

It was at Corinth that **Paul** met **Priscilla** and **Aquila** and stayed with them. Although his teaching was opposed in the synagogue, Paul stayed in Corinth for eighteen months, founding the church to which he subsequently wrote the two letters to the Corinthians.

CYPRUS

An island in the eastern Mediterranean, equidistant from the coasts of Turkey and Syria. In New Testament times it was a Roman province governed by a proconsul. Cyprus became a significant area in the Bronze Age as it was a primary source of copper. The culture was influenced over the centuries .by the Minoans and Myceneans. In the ninth century BC the island was settled by Phoenicians, and it was conquered by the Egyptians in the sixth century. It became part of the Persian empire in 525 BC, fell to Alexander in 333 BC, and became a Roman province in 58 BC. Cyprus is now an independent republic within the Commonwealth, with a majority Greek and minority Turkish population.

In the Old Testament, Cyprus (Chittim in older translations) is briefly referred to in the books of Isaiah, Jeremiah, and Ezekiel. The New Testament apostle **Barnabas** was a native of Cyprus (Acts 4:36), and he traveled there with **Paul** at the start of their first missionary journey, when they encountered the sorcerer Bar-jesus (Acts 13:2–12). After the disagreement between Paul and Barnabas over **Mark**, Barnabas and Mark traveled again to Cyprus.

EPHESUS

Ancient city and capital of Roman province of Asia. It was situated at the mouth of the river Cayster, on the west coast of what is now Asiatic Turkey. The city was established in the tenth century BC, although there was already a settlement there. From ancient times the area had been associated with the worship of a fertility goddess, who later became identified with Artemis (or Roman Diana). The city was conquered by Croesus in the sixth century BC and came variously under Lydian and Persian domination until Alexander established democratic government in 334 BC. Ephesus was finally

Top left Remains of a temple at Corinth, showing the columns which have taken their name from the city

Bottom left A nineteenth-century engraving of the site of the Areopagus in Athens, where Paul preached one of his most famous sermons

Right Roman amphitheater on the island of Cyprus, which was a Roman province in New Testament times

Left The ancient city of Ephesus flourished under the Romans, but has long been uninhabited. The photo reproduced here shows the remains of the great library at Ephesus

Right The seven churches of Asia mentioned in Revelation 1. John was on the island of Patmos when he received the revelation

conquered by the Romans, under whose rule the city flourished. It declined after the fourth century AD and has been uninhabited for centuries.

Paul, with **Priscilla** and **Aquila**, helped to establish the church at Ephesus (Acts 18:19–28, 19:1–10). The popularity of Christianity caused trouble among those who made their living from the cult of Diana, and they stirred up a riot in the city (Acts 19:23–41). After Paul departed from Ephesus (Acts 20:17–38), he left **Timothy** in charge (1 Tim. 1:3). Paul wrote a letter to the church at Ephesus and it was one of the seven Asian churches which received a message in Revelation (Rev. 2:1–7).

HARAN

Haran, or Harran, was an ancient city on the main route from **Nineveh** to Aleppo. The name means "cross-roads" and its position gave it strategic importance. Its name appears in texts from 2000 BC and it later became an important Assyrian center. It was sacked in 763 BC, but was rebuilt and became the last capital of Assyria after the fall of Nineveh. It was then captured by the Babylonians, and was under Roman, then Islamic domination before it fell into ruins. The site is about twenty miles south-east of Urfa in modern Turkey.

Haran was a staging post in **Abraham**'s journey from **Ur** to **Canaan** (Gen. 11:31–12:5). It was the home of **Rebekah** (Gen. 24) and of her nieces, **Rachel** and **Leah**, who both became **Jacob**'s wives in Haran (Gen. 29–31). All Jacob's sons, except Benjamin, were born in Haran.

LYSTRA

A remote town in a mountainous region of the Roman territory of Lycaonia. The region is mentioned by writers from the fourth century BC, and became a Roman province in Pompey's time. The people spoke a distinct language, which was still used in Lystra when **Paul** visited it. The site of the town is near the modern Hatunsaray in Turkey.

Paul and **Barnabas** fled to Lystra when threatened with persecution in Iconium. When Paul healed a crippled man, the people of Lystra mistook the apostles for gods, but their veneration turned to persecution after Paul explained their mistake (Acts 14:6–19). Paul later returned to Lystra, where he circumcised **Timothy** (Acts 16:1–3).

MACEDONIA

An important Roman province and former imperial power. The province covered what is now northern Greece, southern Yugoslavia, and Albania. The Macedonian empire was founded by Alexander in the fourth century BC, but the region came under the

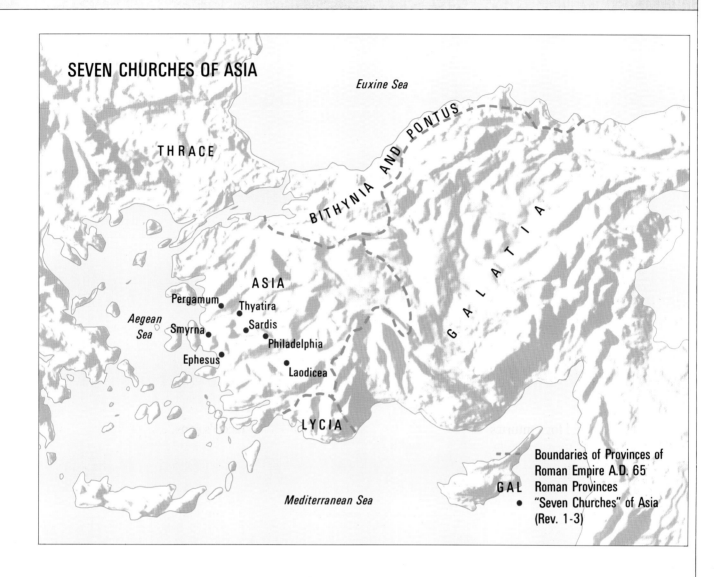

SEVEN CHURCHES OF ASIA

Euxine Sea

THRACE

BITHYNIA AND PONTUS

ASIA

GALATIA

Aegean
Sea

Pergamum
Thyatira
Smyrna
Sardis
Philadelphia
Ephesus
Laodicea

LYCIA

Mediterranean Sea

Boundaries of Provinces of
Roman Empire A.D. 65
GAL Roman Provinces
● "Seven Churches" of Asia
(Rev. 1-3)

control of the Romans in 146 BC.

Paul had a vision of a man from Macedonia, asking him to come and help him (Acts 16:9) and he and Silas immediately went there. He later returned (Acts 20:1–2); and the church established in Macedonia gave financial support to the **Jerusalem** church (Rom. 15:26; 2 Cor. 8:1–4).

> *Intense study of the Bible will keep any man from being vulgar in point of style.*
> SAMUEL TAYLOR COLERIDGE 1772–1834

PHILIPPI

One of the principal cities of the Roman province of Macedonia. It was situated on a steep hill on what is now the River Angista in north-east Greece. The town was developed by Philip of Macedon who conquered it in about 360 BC. It was taken by the Romans in 168 BC and in New Testament times had been colonized by Italians who were given special rights and privileges. The site is now uninhabited but ruins of an amphitheater and temple remain.

Philippi was the first European city to be evangelized by **Paul**. His first visit there was marked by the conversion of **Lydia**, and the imprisonment and miraculous deliverance of Paul and Silas (Acts 16:12–40). Paul's letter to the Philippians thanks them for a gift sent to him in prison.

BIBLIOGRAPHY

Benet, W.R. *The Reader's Encyclopedia* 2nd ed. (A and C Black 1965)

Encyclopaedia Britannica 14th ed. (1937)

Guinness Book of Records 28th ed. (Guinness Superlatives 1982)

Illustrated Bible Dictionary (IVP 1980)

Lang, J.S. *The Complete Book of Bible Trivia* (Tyndale House 1988)

Lockyer, H. *All the Men of the Bible* (Zondervan 1958)

Lockyer, H. *All the Women of the Bible* (Zondervan 1958)

Manser, M.H. *Lion Concise Book of Bible Quotations* (Lion 1982)

Millard, A. *Treasures from Bible Times* (Lion 1985)

INDEX

ACKNOWLEDGEMENTS

Quarto would like to thank the following for their help with this publication and for permission to reproduce copyright material.
Key: *a* = above, *b* = below, *l* = left, *r* = right, *c* = centre, *back* = background.

Jacket photographs (clockwise from top left): Michael Freeman, Susan Griggs Agency, Bridgeman Art Library, Bridgeman Art Library, CM Dixon, Bridgeman Art Library.

6 *a l* CM Dixon
9 Sonia Halliday Photographs
10-11 Barnaby's Picture Library
12 Bridgeman Art Library
13 Bridgeman Art Library
14 Bridgeman Art Library
15 Bridgeman Art Library
16 Bridgeman Art Library
18 E T archive
19 Walter Rawlings
20 Mary Evans Picture Library
21 *a* Sonia Halliday Photographs, *b* Peter Clayton
23 *b* BIPAC, *inset* Peter Clayton
24 Bridgeman Art Library
28 *l* Bridgeman Art Library, *r* C M Dixon
29 Bridgeman Art Library
33 Bridgeman Art Library
35 Bridgeman Art Library
38 *l* C M Dixon, *r* Bridgeman Art Library, *back* Mary Evans Picture Library
39 Werner Forman Archive
41 Bridgeman Art Library
42-43 E T archive
44 *l* and *r* Bridgeman Art Library
45 Bridgeman Art Library
46 Ardea, *back* C M Dixon

47 *a* and *b* C M Dixon
48 Bridgeman Art Library
50 Mary Evans Picture Library
51 Bridgeman Art Library, *back* Mary Evans Picture Library
52-53 Mary Evans Picture Library
54 *l* and *a* Sonia Halliday Photographs, *b* Robert Harding Associates
56-57 Bridgeman Art Library
58 Christie's Colour Library
60-61 Bridgeman Art Library, *back* Mary Evans Picture Library
63 Bridgeman Art Library
65 Jamie Simson
66-67 Ardea, *back* Mary Evans Picture Library
68 *l* Interfoto Picture Library, *r* Ardea, *back* Mary Evans Picture Library
70 Mary Evans Picture Library
71 CM Dixon
72-73 Bridgeman Art Library
74 The National Gallery, London
76-77 Bridgeman Art Library
79 *l* CM Dixon, *r* Bridgeman Art Library
80-81 Bridgeman Art Library
82 CM Dixon
83 Bridgeman Art Library
84-85 Bridgeman Art Library
86 Bridgeman Art Library
88 *l* CM Cixon, *r* Bridgeman Art Library
89 *l* and *r* Barnaby's Picture Library
89 Barnaby's Picture Library

90 Bridgeman Art Library
94-95 Bridgeman Art Library, *back* Mary Evans Picture Library
97 *l* and *r* Bridgeman Art Library
99 *l* and *r* Bridgeman Art Library
101 *a* CM Dixon, *b* Bridgeman Art Library
102 *a* and *b* Fine Art Photographs
105 The National Gallery, London
106 *a* E T archive, *l* Bridgeman Art Library, *r* Adam Woolfitt, Susan Griggs Agency
107 *l* Bridgeman Art Library, *r* Fine Art Photographs
108 *l* and *r* Bridgeman Art Library, *back* Mary Evans Picture Library
109 E T archive
110 Bridgeman Art Library
111 *a* Bridgeman Art Library, *b* CM Dixon
112 Bridgeman Art Library
113 E T archive
115 *a* E T archive, *b* Walker Art Gallery, *back* Mary Evans Picture Library
116-117 Bridgeman Art Library
118-119 *l* CM Dixon, *r* Bridgeman Art Library
120-121 Bridgeman Art Library
122 *l* and *b* CM Dixon, *r* Bridgeman Art Library, *back* Mary Evans Picture Library
123 Bridgeman Art Library
124-125 Bridgeman Art Library
126 Bridgeman Art Library
127 CM Dixon

128 *l* E T archive, *r* BIPAC, *back* Mary Evans Picture Library
129 *l* CM Dixon, *c* Bridgeman Art Library, *r* CM Dixon
130 Bridgeman Art Library
131 Mary Evans Picture Library
132 Michael Freeman
135 Bridgeman Art Library
138 Bridgeman Art Library
139 *l* and *r* BIPAC/Klaus-Otto Hundt, *b* Bridgeman Art Library
140 Michael Freeman
141 *l* BIPAC, *r* Christie's Colour Library
142 *l* Greg Evans Photo Library, *r* Mary Evans Picture Library
143 Alain le Garsmeur/Impact Photos
144 BIPAC/Klaus-Otto Hundt
145 Bridgeman Art Library
146 Greg Evans Photo Library
147 Greg Evans Photo Library
149 Alain le Garsmeur/Impact Photos
150 *a* E T archive, *b* CM Dixon
151 Bridgeman Art Library
152 *a* Jamie Simson, *b* Mary Evans Picture Library
153 Greg Evans Photo Library
154 Bridgeman Art Library

Every effort has been made to trace and acknowledge all copyright holders. Quarto would like to apologise if any omissions have been made.